MAI]

BEYOND PANCAKES

A Collection of 179 Favored Maple Recipes from Maine Cooks and Chefs

Written and compiled by
Elizabeth G. Hodgkins

Maine Maple Producers Association
Skowhegan, Maine

Printed at
Ink Blot Printing
Vassalboro, Maine

Designed by Ginny Raye

Sketches by Earle Mitchell

Cover photography by John Hodgkins

Maine Maple Producers Association
P.O. Box 471
Skowhegan, Maine 04976
www.mainemapleproducers.com

ISBN-13: 978-0-9792729-0-5
ISBN-10: 0-9792729-0-4

TABLE OF CONTENTS

A message from the president 7

Acknowledgements 8

Introduction 9

Maple Savvy

    Maple Producers Lingo 13

    The Maple Advantage 14

    Comparisons 15

    Conversions 15

    What to Buy 16

    Storage 18

    Value-Added Maple Products 19

    When and Where to Buy Maine Maple 19

    Making Pure Maine Maple Syrup 22

A Short History of Maple Syrup 24

I. Toppings, Glazes, Sauces, Spreads 27

II. Appetizers 39

III. Beverages 45

IV. Cereals 54

V. Breads 59

VI. Meat, Fish, and Poultry 84

VII. Baked Beans, Soups, and Main Dishes 104

VIII. Vegetables 116

IX. Salads 127

X. Desserts 141

XI. Maple Nibbles 178

XII. Pancakes 184

Index 194

A MESSAGE FROM THE PRESIDENT

Just the thought of pure Maine maple syrup brings to mind years gone by for many of us. Maybe the memory is the steamy aroma of a pot of boiling sap on the kitchen stove, or perhaps a trip to a local sugarhouse for a fresh taste straight from the evaporator, or grandma's pancakes drizzled with the delicious, all-natural treat.

The Maine Maple Producers Association is pleased that Beth has collected recipes from all over Maine and written *Maine Maple Beyond Pancakes* to help us promote an awareness of our fine maple syrup beyond the walls of our local sugarhouses. You'll find tantalizing recipes for every setting—the family kitchen, the formal dining room, and the niches of professional cooks and chefs everywhere.

Whether you are a first-time user or, like many of us, can't imagine a meal without maple syrup, you will find new and exciting ways to cook with maple in *Maine Maple Beyond Pancakes*. Each recipe, several with their own story, has its unique flavor and pleasant aroma. Make these recipes your own, enjoy reading tidbits about our passionate sugarmakers, visit our sugarhouses, and create your own maple stories and traditions.

May you delight in using pure Maine maple syrup in your kitchen as much as we enjoy producing it.

Michael Bryant, President
Maine Maple Producers Association
www.mainemapleproducers.com

MANY THANKS TO

Val Vaughan for her editing expertise and enthusiasm,

Mary Webber for her valuable words of wisdom, advice, and support for the project,

Penny Savage and Pat Jillson for their time, advice, and encouragement,

Patti Hodgkins for translating into French our request to the French-speaking producers in northwestern Maine for recipes,

The Dominican Sisters of Sabattus for translating into English the recipes submitted in French,

Earle Mitchell for his artwork,

Mike Bryant of MMPA for final details,

The Maine Maple Producers Association for their contributions and sponsorship,

The Central Maine Writers Network for listening to my stories,

Many friends and family who graciously accepted invitations to dine at our home and devoured my trial maple bakes without wincing, and

My dear husband, John, my right hand assistant, and who, many years ago, indulged me with an abundance of the blue ribbon ingredient—our pure Maine maple syrup—that fostered my interest and curiosity in cooking with maple.

P.S. Recipes without credit given came from the author's kitchen.

INTRODUCTION
Why This Collection of Recipes?

"I'm a gentleman farmer, too," boasts John in answer to a question I asked him on our first date some forty years ago.

"A gentleman farmer?" I silently ponder. My mind races: my roots are grounded in the cow pasture of a dairy farm, and our neighbors raise pullets. I recall long journeys through the Haynesville Woods into Aroostook County to visit family friends — potato farmers. I know orchardists, vegetable growers, and sheep herders. There are horse farms. But a gentleman farmer? Besides, the farmers I know have calloused hands, muscled biceps, sunburned noses, and yawn all evening from long hours of manual labor. Not so with John.

He reads my puzzled face. "Oh, I'm just a part-timer," he says. " My cousins, Brud and Bill, and I make maple syrup in Temple during the spring and my ancestors were all farmers and backyard maple producers. I find satisfaction in carrying on the tradition; it's part of my heritage."

"Hmmm." My mind shifts gears again, this time back to the days of my youth. I hear my grandfather call from the dinner table. (We had dinner at noon on the farm and supper at night. Lunch was what we took to school in our lunchboxes.) "Ma, get me that jug of sap from the refrigerator, will ya?" Dressed in a calico housedress, bibbed apron, and black-laced pumps, Grammie bustles from the pantry with his half-gallon jug and sets it by his glass. It's his choice of mealtime beverage during sugaring season. My stomach turns icky at the thought.

Another shift: I see Uncle Harold hunched over his backyard fire. Rocks from a nearby stonewall circle the flame and support a large flat pan billowing steam into the dusk amidst sweet maple aroma. Inside the farmhouse, Aunt Louise stands at the old-fashioned cookstove, flipping pancakes the exact size of her twelve-inch iron skillet. My cousins, my brothers, and I eagerly gather around the family table joking, teasing, giggling, waiting to pig out, oblivious to the hours of work our elders have spent to prepare our favorite Sunday night supper—pancakes lathered with peanut butter and pooled in pure maple syrup.

My dad had no maple trees on our farm, but he insisted that we buy an annual supply of pure maple syrup from a nearby producer, and now I picture metal gallon cans, heavy with pure maple syrup, lining the edge of our cellar stairs. I imagine his plate stacked with pancakes dripping with peaches, strawberries, or applesauce, and drenched with pure Maine maple syrup. "You've done it again, Wilma. What a feast!" he praises my mother between smacking lips.

I had devoured many maple-sweetened breakfasts and Sunday suppers in my youth. When John tells me he has his own sugar shack, I think—so he makes maple syrup? Gee, he'd make a sweet catch!

Well, the gentleman farm operation became a major education for me! The backyard kettle I envisioned is a huge evaporator in a huger sap house accessible only by hiking a mile from the nearest dirt road up a mountainside. Three thousand metal buckets replace the dozen glass jugs of my girlhood, and a Caterpillar tractor and sled the yoke Uncle Harold used to collect the sap. Instead of making three gallons, John and his cousins make 300 gallons. WOW!

Over the next forty years this operation, known as Jackson Mountain Farm, moves twice, downsizes, modernizes and eventually locates on a hillside about a mile from the village. My connection with the maple business also changes from an amazed observer to a dedicated partner.

I also become one of its major consumers. Not only do I whip up a stack of pancakes every Sunday morning for our growing family, I start messing around in the kitchen—experimenting with maple syrup as an ingredient. John's Aunt Marion gives me a small cookbook with intriguing maple recipes, and I just have to try them, and try again; and by jingo, I get hooked. I quickly discover maple not only sweetens, it enhances, flavors, caramelizes, thickens, and glazes foods, as well as delights the partaker! The recipes become favorites, tried and true.

"You must love to cook, Beth," one of my friends observes.

"Not really," I return. "I guess I just love to eat yummy foods that are healthy for me." If I cook and bake from scratch, I have control over the ingredients: unbleached or whole grain flour instead of white flour, canola oil for shortening when possible, pure maple syrup for a sweetener when appropriate. I can substitute, leave out and add; and I can toss in nuts, seeds, raisins, and craisins for extra nutrition. And I can add chocolate chips for fun.

I also find myself practicing frugality—my Scottish heritage— as I plan my weekly menus. By planning ahead, it's easy to disguise leftovers in second preparations, rather than feed them to the electric pig. I cook and bake because the food tastes better, it's made with healthier and more natural ingredients, and the price is right. I find much gratification in preparing a deliciously healthy home-cooked meal and sharing it with my family and friends. Knowing how to use maple syrup to enhance my cooking truly makes a difference.

Why do I put together this collection of recipes called *Maine Maple Beyond Pancakes*? Well, a few years ago I awoke to a swirling snowstorm outside the bedroom window, school was canceled, and I found myself half-listening to the storm reports on the local television station, while I sipped my morning coffee and skimmed the daily newspaper.

"This is the perfect morning to sit around the kitchen table and enjoy a leisurely breakfast of pancakes and Vermont maple syrup," the voice from the television blares.

"Whoops! What did I just hear? A Maine weather forecaster recommending that Maine listeners indulge in Vermont maple syrup? Oh, my! What a faux pas!" My brain makes a note: educate.

Then, a year or so later, I overhear an acquaintance, who has just received a quart of Maine maple syrup as a Christmas gift. She remarks, "You mean I have to go back to eating all those pancakes? I gave them up, when I started this diet." My brain makes another note: education needed.

Comments like these inspired me to compile and write *Maine Maple Beyond Pancakes*, to share a collection of tasty maple recipes, and to educate and entertain fellow citizens of Maine and beyond with some Maine maple wisdom.

First, Maine's annual production of pure maple syrup—more than 250,000 gallons—ranks second among the United States. And Somerset County in northwestern Maine produces more pure maple syrup than any other county in our nation. So please enjoy a stormy morning breakfast, or any leisurely breakfast, dinner, or supper with a stack of warm pancakes (choose one from our mouth-watering collection), and simply pour on the Maine maple syrup!

Second, you don't have to just eat "all those pancakes" to empty a jug of Maine maple syrup. Of course, topping your pancakes, waffles, and French toast with the golden liquid is, undoubtedly, the most popular and traditional use. In fact, it may be the only use you know. However, now you can choose from other, lesser known Maine maple recipes beyond pancakes that I, with the help of two other Maine maple producers, Penny Savage and Pat Jillson, have collected from members of the Maine Maple Producers Association (MMPA), the Southern Maine Maple Syrup Association (SMMSA), the University of Maine Cooperative Extension in Orono, family, friends, and local chefs. Try our recipes for breads, salads and dressings, meats, fish, poultry, baked beans, vegetables, appetizers, toppings, desserts …

You'll get hooked and your jug of pure Maine maple syrup will quickly disappear. You'll need and want another! And once you get the hang of it, you will create and concoct your own recipes.

Just remember the good part: maple has its own character. Because of its chemical composition, maple reacts differently when combined with various foods. It blends spices, mellows acids, cuts vinegars, enhances fats, thickens juices when heated, and seasons whole grains, as well as acts as a subtle sweetener. There is no other ingredient that is comparable. As Eric Ellis, a Maine producer replied when I asked him for a recipe, "I don't really have a recipe. I dump a little here and give a little splash there and savor the difference." Enjoy.

MAPLE SAVVY

MAINE MAPLE PRODUCERS' LINGO

Boiling-off: the evaporation process of syrup making.

First run: the very first sap run of the season, usually has the highest concentration of sugar and produces syrup of the lightest color.

Fresh run: the run of the day.

Saphouse: the rustic building in which the evaporation process of sap takes place. (Sugarhouse and sugarshack are synonymous terms used in other parts of the country.)

Sugarbush: a stand of sugar maples.

Sugaring: a term used for working on any phase of syrup making.

Sugaring-off: the final few seconds; the sap is syrup now; draw it off; get it off the fire!

THE MAPLE ADVANTAGE

Why use pure Maine maple syrup or pure Maine maple sugar? Are there any advantages over white sugar?

Pure Maine maple syrup and pure Maine maple sugar are natural and organic foods processed by heating pure maple sap, a nutrient liquid used by the maple tree during its yearly growth. Since the sap retains these nutrients throughout the evaporation process pure maple syrup and maple sugar supply nutrition to the human body as well. However, there will be slight differences in the products' nutritive compositions and tastes depending on the soils and geographic area in which the sugarbush is located.

The sugars in the products are a source of energy and heat for our bodies. Sucrose is the main sugar found in the lighter amber syrups, while fructose and glucose appear in darker amber syrups in small and variable amounts.

Also, several minerals and vitamins, essential to healthy living, have been identified as being present: potassium, calcium, phosphorus, manganese, iron, and magnesium as minerals, vitamins B2 (riboflavin), B5 (pantothenic acid), measurable amounts of niacin with traces of B6 (pyridoxine), biotin, and folic acid. There are also traces of many amino acids, the building blocks of proteins.

In addition to pure Maine maple syrup and maple sugar being natural and organic, and containing a variety of nutrients, they add a distinct flavor and character to your meals that enhance the quality of life. And as the old timer offers, "Ain't nothin' so good but maple makes it better."

Reference:
"Nutritional Value of Maple Syrup" from *National Maple Syrup Digest* By Maria F. Morselli 1975
Revised by Henry J. Marckres (2003)

COMPARISONS

Sweetner 1/4 cup	Calcium mg	Iron mg	Potassium mg	Calories
Maple Syrup	83	1.0	150	200
Maple Sugar	45	.08	137	176
White Sugar	1	0	2	192

CONVERSION

To experiment with your own recipes, use the following guide to substitute pure Maine maple syrup for white sugar:

1. Use ¾ cup of pure maple syrup for each cup of sugar. Then decrease the dominant liquid (milk or water) in your recipe by 3 tablespoons. Remember maple syrup is sweeter than sugar and is liquid. This ratio will vary with some recipes, and may require adjustment based on results.

2. Add ¼ to ½ teaspoon baking soda to dry ingredients. Maple syrup has a slight acidity which needs to be neutralized for the batter to rise and form properly. DO NOT add baking soda if the recipe calls for buttermilk, sour milk, or sour cream. These ingredients do the neutralizing naturally.

3. Also, your baked goods will brown and bake quicker, when using maple syrup. You should decrease oven temperature by 25 degrees. Maple syrup tends to caramelize, burn on top and edges of baked goods.

References:
   1.*Secrets Of Fat Free Baking* by Sandra Woodruff, RD
      Avery Publishing, Garden City Park, NY, c. 1995
   2.Cooking with Maple Syrup www.yankeegrocrey.com

WHAT TO BUY

So now you know that Maine produces maple syrup of the highest quality, about 250,000 gallons annually, and that its distinct flavor and character, plus its nutrients—called the Maple Advantage—will enhance your cooking. "But," you exclaim, "I don't know what to buy! I hear terms like 'fancy syrup,' 'dark syrup,' 'cooking syrup'. Which is the best? Also, I see it packaged in many different containers. What should I buy?"

Grades

Well, all commercially licensed Maine maple producers must grade their syrup according to federal and state grading standards, if selling it commercially. To grade syrup, a producer pours a small amount of fresh syrup into a clear glass bottle, holds the bottle to a light, and compares the color to sample colors in a standard grading kit to determine the grade. In other words, it is graded according to its color. Hence, we see containers of maple syrup labeled Light Amber, Medium Amber, Dark Amber, or Extra Dark Amber; or we hear them in conversation, referring to the grade of Maine-produced pure maple syrup.

Light Amber syrup is naturally the lightest colored grade. It is usually produced near the beginning of the sugaring season when the sap is sweetest and doesn't require as much time to boil down to the proper density and temperature for syrup. Light Amber syrup has a very delicate maple flavor, and it is beautifully served from a clear glass pitcher or glass jug. Some folks think this is the best tasting and highest grade of syrup. And it's a must for making maple candy.

Medium Amber syrup is called by many their favorite table syrup. Slightly darker than the lighter amber syrup, yet beautifully served as well, Medium Amber syrup is a bit stronger flavored. It is great for pouring on your pancakes, waffles, French toast, hot cereal, grapefruit, ice-cream, and the like.

Dark Amber and Extra Dark Amber syrups are darker and stronger tasting yet. But they, too, are used as table syrup. It's a matter of preference. Dark Amber syrup is also good for baking, but Maine cooks, who use maple syrup often, prefer Extra Dark Amber syrup for its stronger flavor. These grades are generally produced toward the end of the season when the days and nights are a bit warmer, and the sap has a lesser sugar content. It takes longer to boil down to syrup, thus the darkness.

So which is best? That's for you to decide. Your choice! It's all a matter of taste and presentation. "But," you ask, "Does it make a difference what container I buy it in?"

Containers

Maple producers have the option of packaging their syrup in a variety of materials—plastic, glass, or metal— sizes and shapes. Most producers choose to put their syrup into high-density plastic syrup jugs. These containers are the most popular for several reasons: lightweight and non-breakable are the most obvious. Plastic containers are also easier to handle, clean, and ship. Plastic containers are said to retain the syrup's flavor better than metal. The plastic may breathe air, however, which will darken the lighter syrups a bit over a three-month or so period if the syrup is not kept cool; but they are the most economical syrup containers, and, at the same time, make an attractive package perfect for gift-giving.

Some producers package their syrup in metal containers of different shapes and sizes, often with attractive sugaring scenes painted or screened on them. These tins travel well, do not break, and, unlike plastic, do not breathe; however, they are a bit heavier, thus more costly to ship.

High-density plastic jugs and metal tins are available in all the common sizes—gallon, half-gallon, quart, pint, and half-pint. Of course, syrup by the gallon is the most economical way to buy it.

Fancy clear-glass bottles have become very popular in recent years. They are available in a myriad of different shapes and sizes, their amber contents simply irresistible! What could be more eye-catching than a maple leaf radiating golden hues of pure, light-amber Maine maple syrup?

Syrup in clear glass makes the perfect hostess gift or tasty present for friends and relatives at birthday and holiday time. Also, small bottles of sparkling syrup make special favors for guests attending a wedding reception or other parties. Just keep in mind that the glass containers are more expensive and may break in transit.

Suggestion: After emptying clear-glass syrup containers, or plastic jugs, reuse them as vases for cut flowers. Or display the glass container filled with colored water to match your décor on a shelf or in a sun-filled window.

Need to ship a gift of packaged pure Maine maple syrup? Ask your producer for a shipping carton just the right size for your container.

STORAGE

Store unopened syrup in a dark, cool place or pop it into the freezer where it will keep for a long time. Once opened, it must be kept in the refrigerator or freezer. Since a gallon jug takes a good-sized chunk of a refrigerator shelf, I fill a quart jar or jug to store in the refrigerator for quick and convenient use, and tuck the gallon jug into the freezer. When my quart jug is about empty, I remove the gallon jug from the freezer, set it in the sink, and let it defrost until thawed enough to pour. Then I refill the quart jug and return the gallon jug to the freezer.

Mold

If mold should happen to form on the top of your stored syrup, don't panic! Simply bring the syrup to a boil in a pan, remove it from heat, and skim off the mold or strain the syrup through cheesecloth or the like. Pour the syrup into a clean container or jar. Return it to the refrigerator, unless sealed. The syrup will be like new: safe and ready to use!

Crystallization

If the syrup crystallizes at the bottom of the container, just set the container into very hot water until the crystals dissolve and the syrup is pourable again.

VALUE-ADDED MAPLE PRODUCTS

A few Maine maple producers add value to their Light Amber syrup by further processing the syrup to create other maple products, such as maple sugar, maple cream, maple butter, or maple candy. If you are interested in purchasing such products, look on the Maine Maple Producers Association web-site www.mainemapleproducers.com for the names of producers who have them for sale.

WHEN AND WHERE TO BUY MAINE MAPLE

Now that you know what grade or grades to buy, what sizes you want, what kind of containers are available, and that a few producers offer maple value-added products, where can you buy this delectable stuff?

Shopping in the local grocery store one January morning, I meet my neighbor pondering the vast array of pure maple syrup products offered. "I know a little bit about maple syrup, that there are different grades and such," she says to me. "These jugs are all labeled Dark Amber. Where can I find Light Amber?"

Of course, if it had been in March or April, I would have suggested she stop at my house for some fresh run syrup. However, it was January, and we were sold out of the previous season's Light Amber syrup.

So, what should you do to insure that your preferred grade of Maine maple syrup is in your cupboard throughout the year? There are two best bets.

First, check the list of licensed Maine Maple Producers on the web www.mainemapleproducers.com for names, addresses, e-mails, and telephone numbers of Maine maple producers. Some producers have their own web page with further information about their products. (No computer? Phone numbers and addresses are at the end of this section. The Department of Agriculture will assist you.) A maple producer might live close to you. If the producer does not have what you want, he undoubtedly knows someone who does. Many producers will ship their products for cost of shipping, plus cost of carton.

Since many smaller producers run out of syrup before the next season's run, I suggest that you contact a nearby producer early— during late winter or early spring—and order whatever you'll need for the coming year. Be sure to specify the grade and the size and kind of container, keeping in mind that small producers may not offer a large choice. However, if you have a special request, be sure to ask, as they often can meet your needs if they know them ahead of time.

It's generally less expensive, too, to buy directly from the producer, so don't forget to order any gifts that you might want for that hard-to-shop-for person on your Christmas or birthday list. A couple of extra jugs are handy to have for that unanticipated present later in the year. And don't forget to ask for mailing cartons, if you will need them.

The second best bet—and the most fun—is to gather the family, the neighbors, or just hop into the car yourself on the fourth Sunday of March, Maine Maple Sunday, and head for one or several of your area's saphouses. The open saphouses usually advertise in the local newspaper, on the local radio station, or you'll find them listed on the Department of Agriculture's web site, www.getrealgetmaine.com. Check the opening times and enjoy tours of their sugarbushes, savor the aroma of the steam, drink warm syrup, taste samples of tantalizing maple goodies, and immerse yourself in the ambience of the maple heritage dating back to colonial days. Some of the houses even serve a meal, often a pancake breakfast, for a reasonable price. And, of course, they will have fresh Maine maple syrup and possibly other maple products for sale, also.

Late March and Maine Maple Sunday . . . what could be a better way to celebrate end of winter and the coming of spring than exploring a sugarbush! Wear your boots and warm clothing. It's great family fun!

Other outlets for pure Maine maple syrup and value-added products include weekly local farmers' markets in towns and cities, roadside farmstands throughout the state, and some of the agricultural county fairs late summer and fall. Most health food stores carry pure maple products and recently I have noticed that some of the major grocery store chains carry pure Maine maple syrup now. (Be sure to read labels at the grocery store to make sure you are buying pure maple syrup.)

For those wanting more information, see the Maine Maple Producers Association website, www.mainemapleproducers.com or contact the Maine Department of Agriculture, who are very helpful in matters of Maine agriculture, at the addresses shown below, or visit its website at www.getrealgetmaine.com.

Maine Department of Agriculture
Food and Rural Resources
Office of Commissioner
28 State House Station
Augusta, ME 04333
Telephone: 207-287-3871

Maine Department of Agriculture
Division of Market & Production Development
28 State House Station
Augusta, ME 04333-0028

MAKING PURE MAINE MAPLE SYRUP

"How do you make maple syrup, anyway?" I often hear people ask. Well, to put it simply, maple syrup is the product made by evaporating water from maple sap. The sap is usually syrup when it boils at 219 degrees Fahrenheit and has a sugar density of 59 degrees on the Brix Scale or 32 degrees Baume.

"What is maple sap?" Sap is a clear, watery liquid that is approximately 97% water plus natural sugars, minerals and organic acids. If you taste it, it tastes like slightly sweetened water and that is exactly what it is. However, it is sweetened with natural sugars manufactured by the maple tree only.

When late-winter days warm to above freezing (33 to 40 degrees) after freezing nights (18 to 28 degrees) the sap begins to form. Water and nutrients from the thawing soil start to ooze up the tree trunk through its cell system. As it flows, it absorbs stored sugars from the photosynthesis process of the previous growing season. The slightly sweetened water, or maple sap, carries nutrients to feed the buds, blossoms, and leaves of the tree. It is this watery and sweetened liquid that maple producers boil down to a certain concentration—a point determined by the Department of Agriculture—of sugar solution.

In late February producers wallow, often on snowshoes, through deep snow or slip and slide on icy crust (usually on a side hill) to drill tap holes, 2½ inches deep, into healthy maple trees that are at least 12 inches in diameter. Larger producers use a power drill. If the trees have a diameter more than 22 inches, they drill two holes into the same tree. Next, spiles, sometimes called spouts, are tapped by hand into the holes to catch the flowing sap and direct the liquid into a bucket or plastic tubing.

The larger commercial producers use a network of plastic tubing strung from tree to tree to collect the sap by gravity flow, though a vacuum pump is often used to increase production of the sap. The plastic tubing method not only eliminates time-consuming and back-breaking collection of sap using buckets, but provides less opportunity for bacterial growth. Thus, a lighter grade of syrup is usually made from sap collected by tubing.

If the producer uses buckets, the sap must be collected on foot, dumped into a large tank usually placed on an old wooden sled and drawn by horses or perhaps a tractor. If the trees are close to the road, however, the farmer uses a truck equipped with a large tank to collect and transport the sap. The sap is stored in a holding tank at the saphouse until the farmer is ready to start the evaporation process.

The sap is boiled in large evaporation pans, called an evaporator, over a wood fire or an oil burner until it reaches about 219 degrees, 7 degrees above the boiling point of water. Then the sugar content is measured exactly with a hydrometer, a hydrotherm, or a refractometer, as altitude and atmospheric pressure can change the boiling point of a liquid. The syrup is then drawn off and filtered to remove nitre, a sugar sand that forms in the final stage of boiling. If it passes the final test—the taste test—it's graded for color and is ready to be canned.

Boiling-off, as it is sometimes called, is a long process. The higher the sugar content in the sap the less time it takes to make syrup. It takes approximately 40 gallons of sap to make a gallon of syrup. Generally, the season lasts from four to six weeks. After the buds on the trees begin to swell, the syrup will acquire a "buddy" taste. Then it's time to pull the taps.

Sugaring is an awesome season, one of a kind. It starts in mid-winter with mounds of snow on the ground and exits with nodding trillium and dancing Dutchman's britches affirming spring has come!

If you have never visited a saphouse, I strongly urge you to do so during sugaring time. Maine Maple Sunday, always the fourth Sunday in March, is a great day to do so, but if you see steam rising through the vented rooftop of a saphouse on any day during the season, I'm sure you'd be welcomed and given a grand tour. Revel in the sweet aroma, let the steam curl your hair, ask questions, watch the syrup maker eyeball the draw-off and bob the hydrotherm, empty some buckets, taste the sap, drink the syrup, fill your jug! Experience it all!

A SHORT HISTORY OF MAPLE SYRUP

So you think you know the origin of maple syrup, do you? I thought once, too, that the discovery of maple syrup started with the Iroquois and a broken limb, a hollow rock, and a warm day, or Native children mouthing sap-cicles they had retrieved from a wounded maple branch, or maple sap oozing out of a Tomahawk-slashed tree into a cooking pot placed accidentally at the base. But now, I'm not so sure.

Plimoth Plantation is a living history museum in Plymouth, Massachusetts. Through its living exhibits, it recreates the people and culture of 17th-century Plymouth, specifically 1627, seven years after the Pilgrims landed on a nearby rock. I was there once, November 1978 or so, with my family, and when I discovered the extent of my temporal jump—three hundred and fifty years—I thought, "This may be the place, the place where I can find the answer, where I can learn how maple sugaring *really* started."

I searched there carefully for an informed-appearing Pilgrim, an industrious one who might be explaining his way of life to a group of children, and who might be used to all manner of questions. I approached one wearing a wide-brimmed hat and leggings, and tying together twig reinforcement for an adobe chimney. He introduced himself—a 17th-century name I forget now—and we chatted a moment. Then I asked him, "Have the Indians showed you how to make maple syrup yet?"

"Maple syrup?" he queried.

"Yes, maple syrup from the sap of the maple tree."

"I don't know maple syrup," he said.

"Do you know molasses?" I asked him.

"No, I don't know molasses."

I pursued the subject a bit with him. I knew that cane sugar had not yet reached America, but certainly they must have known some kind of sugar, if not as a sweetener then as a base for rum or some other beverage. "What do you use for sweetener?" I asked.

"Sugar cones. Sugar cones from Barbados," he answered.

"Sugar cones? What are they?"

"They are hard, like rocks, and sweet. We scrape off a bit to sweeten and preserve our fruits."

"But no maple syrup?"

"No."

"And the Indians don't have maple syrup either?"

"I don't see any. We trade them sugar cones."

"Well, be patient," I told him. "Perhaps they will." And perhaps the Indians eventually did share their knowledge with the settlers, but I remain unconvinced that the Natives *discovered* the sweetness in maple sap.

But don't misunderstand me. I think the Natives made and used maple sugar—they still do—they just didn't discover it. The sweetness in maple sap was *shown* to them, passed down you might say. The sweetness in maple sap, I believe, was discovered by the red squirrel, *Tamiasciurus hudsonicus*, the chatterer. The red squirrel dates from the Ice Age, 10,000 years ago, and is known, as I have observed, to chew into maple trees and drink the sap. The red squirrel also chews into maple trees, lets the sap ooze out onto the stem, or a branch, and then returns to devour the residue after evaporation has sweetened it. The red squirrel is the only rodent I have observed harvesting sap—or a modified version of syrup—from a maple tree. And I am sure the Natives made the same observation. After the early work by the red squirrel, the rest was easy.

I have read in some maple manual that maple sugar (and honey) was the sole sweetener in America until cane sugar was introduced in the mid-1600s. But even then, due to its high cost, cane sugar was slow to displace maple sugar. By the 1700s, cane sugar was regularly available everywhere in America, and its popularity had grown considerably in the more genteel households. But, in spite of cane sugar's widespread availability and steady decline in the cost, maple sugar remained America's primary sweetener for longer than one might expect. Mainly because the anti-slavery colonists objected to the misery endured by African slaves on West Indian sugar plantations and boycotted their sugar. So, in colonial farmsteads of the north, the word was passed, "Make your own sugar," and maple sugar remained the sweetener of choice. Production grew to record levels, reaching thirty-five million pounds in 1860.

Following the Civil War, the price of cane sugar continued its steady decline—as did the production of maple sugar—until near the end of the 19th-century when cane sugar cost less to buy than maple sugar did to make. Cane sugar, however, grew scarce and costly again during World War I. In 1918, American maple sugarmakers produced the all-time record American crop of near five million gallons of syrup and twelve million pounds of sugar. This according to the United States Department of Agriculture.

After World War I, cane sugar returned in abundant quantities as an inexpensive sweetener, and maple sugar production began a long decline. By 1951, the production of maple sugar as a commodity had virtually disappeared, and most maple sugarmakers had turned to maple syrup, selling it in cans and bottles mainly as a topping for pancakes and waffles. And the past fifty years or so has seen continued growth in maple syrup production and sales as a delicacy, a unique and flavorful topping.

But there is a world of maple syrup beyond pancakes and waffles, and syrup producers are now promoting its wider use in home kitchens: in breads and beverages, with appetizers and on desserts, in sauces and glazes, and in the tasteful preparation of many other foods and condiments. The short history of maple syrup is being lengthened still.

John Hodgkins
Jackson Mountain Farm, Temple

I

TOPPINGS, GLAZES, SAUCES, SPREADS

The Maine maple producers say pure Maine maple syrup is the shining star of toppings. It's silky smooth texture and natural rich flavor is simply unsurpassed. They have already done the cooking to perfection, so just open the jug and pour it on--pancakes, waffles, French toast, a fresh grapefruit half, hot cereal, warm biscuits, sausage ... and, of course, ice cream!

However, maple syrup added to other ingredients to create toppings, glazes, sauces, and spreads can also embellish and enhance an ordinary food, meal, or dessert. The following pages in Section I include an assortment of scrumptious recipes that will add taste, interest, and elegance to dining.

Read through them, as several complement more than one type of dish. For example a sauce you might choose to accompany a meat dish could taste delicious on a dessert, too. Weird? Yup! But the recipes work. Try them. And don't forget the old timer was right: "Ain't nothin' so good but maple makes it better."

APPLE SAUCE

Apple sauce cooked in maple syrup is a perfect accompaniment to chicken, turkey, pork, ham, fish, toast and peanut butter, or cookies. The maple mellows the flavors of the apples.

8 to 10 tart Maine apples (Cortland or early Macs)
About ¼ cup pure Maine maple syrup (to taste)
About 1/2 cup water

Bring maple syrup and water to boil in a large pot. Meanwhile, wash and chunk apples. Add to boiling mixture and simmer until very tender. Sieve through a food mill for a pureed sauce. The sauce will be a pleasing rosy hue from the apple peels. If you want a chunky sauce; peel, core, and chunk the apples. Then add them to the boiling mixture. Simmer until fork tender. Cool and store in refrigerator or freeze some for later.

Recipe adapted from the *Maple Digest*

CRANBERRY-MAPLE SAUCE

Here is another sauce to serve with meats. The tartness of berries and orange juice is softened with maple sweetness. Oh, so good!

1 pound fresh Maine cranberries
¾ cup orange juice
½-3/4 cup pure Maine maple syrup

Rinse cranberries. Combine with orange juice and maple syrup in saucepan and bring to boil. Simmer until cranberries start to burst. Cool and store in refrigerator.

Submitted by Penny Savage
Mitchell and Savage Maple Syrup, Bowdoin

CRANBERRY-ORANGE-GINGER SAUCE

"Wish I could think of a shorter, zippier name!" says Diana.

The sauce doesn't need a zippy name to give it great color, texture, and extra zing! And it's so versatile. She suggests using it on ice cream, puddings, pumpkin pie, squash, yogurt, ham, or serve with meats as you would plain cranberry sauce.

1 cup white sugar
2 cups water
4 cups fresh or frozen Maine cranberries
1/3 cup orange juice
1/3 cup pure Maine maple syrup (Dark or Extra Dark)
½ tablespoon grated orange zest (colored part of rind only)
1 tablespoon julienne strips of orange zest (colored part of rind)
1½ tablespoons coarsely chopped candied (or fresh) ginger
    or use 1 teaspoon dried ginger (to taste)

Simmer sugar and water in large saucepan over moderately high heat for about 5 minutes, or until liquid just starts to become syrupy. Add the cranberries and simmer another 5 minutes, or until berries begin to pop. Add the orange juice, maple syrup, grated orange zest, strips of orange zest, and ginger and simmer another 2 to 3 minutes.

Pour into sterilized jars and process in boiling bath for 10 minutes or store in refrigerator or freezer.

Makes about 5 cups.

Submitted by Diana Demers
Brambleberry Farms, Weld

ORANGE-MAPLE GLAZE

Use this delish glaze to baste chicken, salmon, pork or ham while grilling, baking, broiling, or sautéing. Omit rosemary, and you have a delightful orange-maple topping to transform the ordinary pudding or plain cake to the extraordinary!

¼ cup pure Maine maple syrup
½ cup fresh orange juice
¼ cup apple cider or apple juice
¼ teaspoon dried rosemary

Over low heat, boil orange juice and cider together in small saucepan for 5 minutes, stirring occasionally. Stir in maple syrup and rosemary. Continue to boil for another 5 minutes, stirring often, until glossy and slightly thickened. This will make enough glaze (approximately ½ cup) for 2 chicken breasts, 1 pound of salmon steaks or fillet, or 2 to 3 pork chops. Baste meat with glaze the last 10 minutes of cooking—be it grilling, baking, broiling, or sautéing. Reserve enough glaze to spoon over meat when ready to serve. Yum!

ORANGE-MAPLE SAUCE

Quick and easy, but so delish! A pleasing sauce for "a second preparation" using sliced pork or chicken.

2 tablespoons pure Maine maple syrup
¼ cup brown sugar
2 tablespoons fresh orange juice

Warm sliced meat, covered, in 350 degree oven. Whisk maple syrup, brown sugar, and orange juice together and warm. Pour over meat. Return to oven and cook, basting occasionally, (2 to 5 minutes) until glaze thickens and coats meat slices.

PINEAPPLE SAUCE

This is a quick make-ahead sauce that adds flavor and texture to your Easter ham while helping to cut the saltiness.

1 can (7 ounce) crushed pineapple
2 tablespoons (or to taste) pure Maine maple syrup

Mix the pineapple and maple syrup together in a small saucepan and cook over low heat, stirring often until slightly thickened. (If you are making this a day or two ahead, store in refrigerator. When near time to serve, zap in microwave until warm.) After the sliced ham is on the serving platter, spoon the sauce over it. Or pour the sauce into a small bowl with ladle and place on the table so guests can serve themselves.

MAPLE-DIJON GLAZE FOR MEATLOAF

A scrumptious topping for any favorite meatloaf recipe. The mixture of sweet maple and Dijon gives the loaf a finishing touch for family or company.

¼ cup pure Maine maple syrup
2 tablespoons Dijon mustard
2 tablespoons ketchup (optional)

Whisk together and brush a thick coat onto meatloaf. Baste occasionally with remaining maple mixture, if desired.

An adaptation from *Jimtown Store Cookbook*
via *The New York Times*

BBQ SAUCE

"Delicious with chicken," writes Sylvie.
Quick and easy.

- 1 cup ketchup
- ½ cup chili sauce
- ½ cup pure Maine maple syrup
- 1 teaspoon oregano
- ¼ teaspoon black pepper
- ¼ teaspoon salt
- 1 clove garlic, finely chopped

Mix all ingredients in saucepan and heat over low heat for about 10 minutes. Store in refrigerator.

Submitted by Sylvie Pare
Dole Pond Maple Products, Quebec

MAPLE-MUSTARD BARBECUE SAUCE

This is a spicy, sweet and sour basting sauce for grilling chicken, pork chops or spare ribs. Makes enough for 4.

- 2 tablespoons Dijon mustard or other strong mustard
- 2 tablespoons lemon juice
- 1 clove garlic, crushed through press
- 1 teaspoon cracked black pepper
- ½ teaspoon dried thyme leaves, crushed
- 1/3 cup pure Maine maple syrup
- 1 tablespoon canola oil

Whisk together all ingredients in order listed. Marinate meat 2 to 3 hours before grilling.

Note: Use this same recipe to glaze ham or roast pork, except omit oil and add 2 teaspoons of grated lemon rind.

MAPLE WALNUT TOPPING

This topping is a very popular item among Diana's family and customers at Brambleberry Farm in Weld. "Use on baked ham, ice cream, bread pudding, or pumpkin pie," she suggests.

"For those with creative dessert ideas that require a sinful topping, here's an option," writes Paul Rossignol, as he describes a similar recipe in his book, Nature's Sweetness.

¼ cup unsalted butter
3 cups coarsely chopped walnuts
1½ cups Extra Dark pure Maine maple syrup
½ cup light corn syrup
1/3 cup water
¼ cup sugar

Melt the butter in a large skillet over low heat. Stir in walnuts, stirring to coat well. Toast walnuts, stirring constantly, until they have absorbed all of the butter and developed a rich, nutty aroma (5 to 7 minutes). Do not allow the butter to brown. Remove from heat and set aside.

In a medium-sized saucepan, combine maple syrup, corn syrup, water, and sugar. Over low heat stir constantly until all the sugar is dissolved. Increase heat to medium and bring to boil. Reduce heat and simmer for 15 minutes, stirring often to prevent sticking. Stir in the toasted walnuts and cook 2 minutes more. Remove from heat.

Ladle into hot jars, leaving ½ inch headspace. Process half pint jars in 200 degree hot water bath for 10 minutes.

Submitted by Diana Demers
Brambleberry Farm, Weld

PEANUT BUTTER SAUCE

Is this without doubt one of the most luscious ice cream sauces ever? My family thinks so! Pure maple syrup and peanut butter make for an interesting blend of favorite flavors.

¾ cup light brown sugar
½ cup whole or skim milk
¼ cup pure Maine maple syrup
1 tablespoon butter
¼ cup crunchy natural peanut butter
½ teaspoon vanilla extract

In a small saucepan stir together sugar, milk, maple syrup, and butter. Cook until mixture starts to boil, stirring constantly over low heat. Remove from heat and add peanut butter and vanilla. Continue to stir until well blended and smooth. Serve warm over vanilla ice cream. Store extra sauce in refrigerator. Makes 1 cup.

Recipe adapted from Beatrice Vaughan's *Maple Cookbook*

RHUBARB SAUCE

The sweet maple mellows the mouth-puckering rhubarb. This sauce completes a delicious shortcake when generously spooned over warmed biscuits and mounded with whipped cream, or spoon it on Maple Gingerbread with whipped cream. Or simply serve with cookies or toast and peanut butter. It's just plain yummy.

4 cups rhubarb, cut into ½ inch pieces
½ cup pure Maine maple syrup
½ cup water

Heat rhubarb, maple syrup, and water until mixture boils. Continue to simmer for about 30 minutes. Store in refrigerator or freezer.

BERRY OR PEACH SAUCE

Lots of delish options! All scrumptious! Use your imagination. Here are some ideas:

1. Serve warm over pancakes or waffles.
2. Dress up a slice of plain cake.
3. Serve warm over ice cream or cream puffs.
4. For a special dessert at brunch, serve a scoop of frozen vanilla yogurt on top of pancakes or a waffle and top with the berry sauce or peaches.

BERRY SAUCE

2 cups hulled and halved fresh or frozen strawberries,
         raspberries, or blueberries, or a combo
2 tablespoons butter
1 teaspoon lemon juice
¼ cup pure Maine maple syrup

In 2-quart saucepan, cook berries in the butter over medium heat for 2 or 3 minutes. Reduce heat to low and add lemon juice and maple syrup. Bring to simmer and cook until berries are tender, about 10 minutes, stirring occasionally. Makes 2½ cups.

WARM PEACH SAUCE

Substitute 2 to 3 peeled and sliced peaches for the berries and place in an oiled baking dish. Combine the melted butter, maple syrup, lemon juice and add ¼ teaspoon cinnamon. Pour over the peaches and bake, covered, in a 375 degree oven for 15 minutes. Uncover and bake 15 minutes longer, basting occasionally.

Note: If using fresh strawberries or raspberries, you may opt for skipping the butter and cooking process. Mash berries and gently mix with lemon juice and maple syrup to taste.

CARAMEL SAUCE

"I especially enjoy this caramel for dipping fresh cut apples or to drizzle over vanilla ice cream," exclaims Eric.

2 cups pure Maine maple syrup
1 tablespoon corn syrup or glucose
6 tablespoons of canned evaporated milk

Coat sides of large saucepan with butter. Slowly heat syrups to 232 degrees. Remove from heat and let stand a few minutes. Add milk. Stir with wooden spoon until color is uniform. Pour into glass jars to store. Let cool. Keep refrigerated.

Submitted by Eric Ellis
Maine Maple Products, Inc. Madison

CHOCOLATE SAUCE

"A delicious dark and semi-sweet topping for ice cream, cakes, cream puffs," writes Penny, "and just to spoon for extra energy!"

6 tablespoons unsweetened cocoa
2 tablespoons butter
½ cup boiling water
1¼ cups pure Maine maple syrup (Dark or Extra Dark)
        or Maine maple sugar (to taste)
1 teaspoon vanilla extract or 2 teaspoons rum

Melt butter with cocoa in top of double boiler. Add boiling water. Stir well and add maple syrup or sugar. Let sauce boil readily, covered, for about 3 minutes. DO NOT STIR. Uncover, reduce heat to low and cook 2 more minutes without stirring. Let cool and add vanilla or rum.

Submitted by Penny Savage
Mitchell and Savage Maple Syrup, Bowdoin

MAPLE BUTTER

A slightly sweetened butter that's, oh, so good warmed and spread on morning toast, hot biscuits, pancakes, waffles, apple pudding, and, yes, gingerbread.

1 cup pure Maine maple syrup
¾ cup butter (not margarine)

Heat maple syrup to 234 degrees on a candy thermometer without stirring. Stir in butter. Allow to cool about 10 minutes; then beat until thick and creamy. Store in refrigerator.

Submitted by Donna Tracy
Maple Hill Farm, Farmington

MAPLE-HONEY BUTTER

Kristi blends her Maine maple syrup, maple sugar, and honey with butter to create an interesting combo of subtle sweetness. Try it on a favorite cracker, hot biscuits, a toasted bagel, a slice of whole grain toast, or even a hot-off-the-grill pancake, waffle, or French toast.

1 cup unsalted butter (2 sticks)
¼ cup pure Maine maple syrup
2 tablespoons pure Maine honey
2-3 tablespoons pure Maine maple sugar (or white sugar will do)

Beat all ingredients together until smooth. Roll in parchment paper or store in a glass jar and refrigerate.

Submitted by Kristi Brannen
Spring Break Maple and Honey, Smyrna

CREAM CHEESE SPREAD

Cream cheese and maple? Delectable! Spread it on breads, toast, bagels, crackers. It also makes an excellent icing for carrot cake.

½ cup pure Maine maple syrup (Dark Amber preferred)
6 ounces cream cheese (at room temperature)

Heat maple syrup in small saucepan and simmer, stirring occasionally, over medium-low heat to 235 degrees on a candy thermometer or until it has thickened to heavy honey consistency. Let cool, stirring once or twice; then beat into the cream cheese. Store it in tightly covered container in refrigerator. It keeps a long time, that is, if you can make it last!

MAPLE CREAM

Another delicious option for that breakfast or brunch mini-bagel, toast tips, or snack crackers.

2 cups pure Maine maple syrup (Light Amber)

Boil maple syrup in large, heavy kettle over medium-high heat to 235 degrees on candy thermometer. Stir occasionally to prevent it from boiling over. Leaving the thermometer in place, put the kettle in cold water to cool rapidly until it reaches room temperature (about 70 degrees). Do not stir while cooling. Remove from cold water and beat until creamy, has formed fine granules, and has thickened. This will take about 20 minutes of stirring by hand, or use electric beater.

Store in glass or plastic container in refrigerator for up to 3 months. If it separates, put in microwave for 10 to 15 seconds and stir. If too thick, stir in a small amount of maple syrup.

Can also store in freezer for up to a year.

University of Maine Cooperative Extension (Both recipes).

II

APPETIZERS

The gracious tradition of serving hors d'oeuvres or appetizers
before a meal has been commonplace in Europe for centuries.
However, the custom is relatively new to our country and Maine.

Naturally, Maine maple cooks have taken advantage of the new
course and have experimented with their prize ingredient to create
tantalizing hors d'oeuvres and appetizers of the highest quality.
They soon discovered that maple pairs well with sour cream, cream
cheese, mayonnaise, and yogurt for vegetable and fruit dips, and
with the saltiness of bacon and sausages. Yum!

Just beware! The serving platters will empty quickly! "Ain't
nothin' so good, but maple makes it better!" the old timer says.

BACON-WRAPPED SCALLOPS

This appetizer is elegantly delicious. Take one and you'll want another, and another!

I recall my first experience with bacon-wrapped scallops. A group of Maine maple producers had gathered around WB51-TV's Jim Crocker, admiring his culinary expertise in front of the cameras. Crocker's first presentation from the oven was a sheet stacked with bacon-wrapped scallops embellished with maple syrup. He pitched a Maine Maple Sunday message to his television audience and then passed the platter of aromatic morsels to the front row of maple producers to "dispose of the evidence." Bob Smith, Al Bolduc, and some others were there. When the platter arrived at my seat in the second row, it was empty. Enough said. You'll love 'em.

Scallops prepared in this manner make a favorite seafood dish for dinner, also.

1 pint fresh sea scallops
½ pound of lean bacon, cut into 4 inch strips
About ¼ cup pure Maine maple syrup
24 toothpicks soaked in water for 5 minutes

Partially cook bacon in a little maple syrup. Wrap scallops with bacon strips and secure with toothpicks. Brush with more maple syrup. Broil or bake, basting with maple syrup and turning until bacon is crisp on all sides. Takes about 10 to 14 minutes. Drain on paper plate or towel. Arrange on platter with parsley and lemon slices.

Submitted by Tony & Irene Couture
Maple Valley Farms, Jay

TOMATO DIP/DRESSING

This bread/vegetable dip is a favorite with our Maine maple producers to the north. Dense whole-grain bread cut into finger-sized breadsticks and dipped into this maple, tomato mixture is delish! Raw veggies are, also.

After sampling this, my imagination turned creatively wild. I took 3 parts of dip, added 2 parts of cider vinegar, and shook it well in a glass jar. Now the dip is a scrumptious dressing for spinach, egg, and bacon salad or to drizzle over a bed of greens.

1 cup tomato ketchup
1 cup vegetable oil (or less, I used ¼ cup)
½ cup pure Maine maple syrup
1 teaspoon dry mustard (or 4 teaspoons Dijon mustard)
2 tablespoons lemon juice
4 teaspoons relish (optional)
1 celery stalk, finely chopped
1 small green onion, finely chopped
    (or substitute dried minced)
1 clove garlic, finely chopped (or substitute garlic powder)
1 tablespoon fresh parsley, finely chopped (optional)

Mix all ingredients in blender or by hand and serve with whole-grain breadsticks, raw vegetables such as cauliflower, broccoli, celery and carrots. It keeps for two weeks stored in the refrigerator. Shake well before using. Makes about 2 ½ cups.

Submitted by Danielle Rodrigue, MMPA and SCS
Sylvie Pare, Dole Pond Maple Products
Martine Pruveau, Mountain Maple Products
Quebec

Chantal Gilbert and Richard Rodrigue, also from Quebec, submitted a variation of this recipe. They omit the oil all together.

RAW VEGGIE DIP

*"Yum. What's in this dip?" I've been asked many times.
A few years ago when I was still teaching, one of my first graders
brought a platter of veggies and this dip for a party treat. Between
the children and me the plate went home empty. Here is my
adapted recipe. Excellent for dipping carrots, celery, peppers,
cucumbers, zucchini, broccoli, cauliflower. This dip, also, is delish
spread on crackers. The maple makes it better!*

1 cup Miracle Whip, low fat
1 cup sour cream or plain yogurt
3 tablespoons catsup
3 tablespoons pure Maine maple syrup
3 tablespoons minced onion
      or 1 tablespoon dried, minced onion
1 teaspoon lemon juice
1 tablespoon curry powder (or to taste—I like 1 teaspoon)

Put all ingredients in blender or whisk by hand until smooth.
Refrigerate overnight.

FRUIT DIP

*A delicately flavored dish for dipping apple or pear slices,
strawberries or any fruit that will dip.*

1 8-ounce package softened cream cheese
½ cup sour cream
¼ cup brown sugar
2 tablespoons pure Maine maple syrup
Beat until smooth.

Submitted by Pip Marrotte, Westbrook
Friend of Mitchell and Savage Maple Syrup

MAINE MAPLE SUNDAY DIP/SPREAD

"Serving snacks with Maine maple syrup at Jackson Mountain Farm on Maine Maple Sunday," are the words that appear in the Franklin Journal the Friday before our sugarhouse will be open to the public for touring our operation and sampling our blue ribbon syrup. "What can I serve to visitors that will be different, catch their attention, whet their palates, and cut the sweetness of the maple sundaes and donuts that I traditionally offer?" I ponder. I flip through my file of recipes for appetizers and come across my adaptation of Clam Diggers Dip that everyone loves. "Ah, that's it, only I'll leave out the clams." On Maple Sunday in the saphouse, I place the bowl of dip on ice and serve crackers instead of veggies to save prep time. Now my veggie dip is a maple spread. It disappears before closing time. It must be the maple!

Here's my adaptation to the original recipe:

> 1 8-ounce package softened cream cheese
> ¼ cup sour cream, or 2 tablespoons of sour cream
>   and 2 tablespoons of Miracle Whip
> 1 clove garlic, finely chopped,
>   or about ½ teaspoon garlic powder (to taste)
> 1 teaspoon dried minced onion (to taste)
> ½ teaspoon Worcestershire sauce
> 2 teaspoons lemon juice
> 2 tablespoons pure Maine maple syrup (to taste)

In a small mixing bowl beat together the cream cheese and sour cream (Miracle Whip, if using) until smooth. Stir in garlic, dried minced onion, Worcestershire sauce, lemon juice, and maple syrup. Cover and chill thoroughly. Serve with fresh veggie sticks, crackers, or chips.

Note: For clam dip, just add a 6-ounce can of minced clams.

MAPLE APPETIZERS

Doesn't this recipe sound palate pleasing?
Perfect for a crowd, or halve it for a small crowd.

1 13½-ounce can pineapple chunks in syrup
2 8-ounce packages brown & serve sausage links
4 teaspoons cornstarch
½ teaspoon salt
½ cup pure Maine maple syrup
1/3 cup water
1/3 cup vinegar
½ cup drained maraschino cherries
1 medium-sized green pepper cut in ¾ inch squares

Drain pineapple, reserving ½ cup liquid. Cut sausages in thirds crosswise and brown. Drain on paper towel. At serving time blend cornstarch, salt, reserved liquid, maple syrup, water and vinegar in a chaffing-like dish. Heat to boiling over direct heat, stirring constantly. Cook and stir a few more minutes. Add drained pineapple, sausage, cherries, and green pepper. Heat through. Keep warm over hot water. To eat, spear with cocktail picks. (For a small crowd, ingredients could be assembled into mini-kabobs ahead of time.)

University of Maine Cooperative Extension, Bangor

MAPLED GRAPEFRIUT

An easy and all-time favorite appetizer or dessert for brunch
or supper.

Drizzle a bit of pure Maine maple syrup over grapefruit halves and top with a maraschino cherry in the centers. Serve cold or brown briefly under broiler. A treat ready to eat!

III

BEVERAGES

"Cups of kindness bring to mind the heart-warming sociability of friends over fragrant, steaming cups of coffee or tea. If the weather is warm, tall frosty glasses of chilled fruit juice take their part in pleasant hospitality."

Betty Crocker
Betty Crocker's Picture Cookbook

Pure Maine maple syrup is a favored ingredient when it comes to whipping up beverages in the kitchen or aging them in the cellar. It lends a mellow sweetness to milk and tea drinks that nourish, relax, and warm our bodies. The acids of citrus, cider, and even vinegar beg for maple to blend their distinct flavors into drinks that quench our thirst in the garden or on the back patio. Also, maple softens the rough edges of the liquor in mixed drinks by naturally blending the various strong flavors.

Here is a variety of recipes for beverages to be served to growing kids and convalescents, to the summer haying crew, to the cocktail party. Be daring and experiment.

MAPLE MILK

A nourishing and tasty treat for the kids, for the convalescents, or for anybody at any time to boost the energy and lift the spirit.

1 cup milk
1 tablespoon pure Maine maple syrup

Mix and enjoy.

Maine Milk Commission

MITCHELL SWITCHELL

"A traditional thirst-quenching drink for hay making on hot summer days," raves Mitch.

½ cup pure Maine maple syrup
¼ cup cider vinegar
1 tablespoon ground ginger (for switchell with a true bite,
    use 2 teaspoons fresh ginger)

Mix maple syrup, cider vinegar, and ginger in small amount of hot water to blend. Add 2 quarts cold water.

Chill and quench your thirst.

Submitted by Earle Mitchell
Mitchell and Savage Maple Syrup, Bowdoin

SUGAR-TIME PUNCH

A favorite from one of our Canadian members whose sugarbush operates in Somerset County, Maine.

1.14 liters white rum
1½ liters (6½ cups + 1 tablespoon) unsweetened orange juice
1½ liters (6 ½ cups + 1 tablespoon) unsweetened grapefruit juice
½ bottle grenadine syrup (375 ml)
1 jar maraschino cherries
3 sliced oranges
2 sliced grapefruits
Pure Maine maple syrup to taste

Mix all ingredients. When ready to serve add ice cubes.

Yield: 5.5 liters (about 6 quarts, or about 1½ gallons)

Submitted by Chantel Gilbert and Richard Rodrigue
Quebec

DOG-DAY LEMONADE

"A real thirst quencher!" Any time!

2 quarts water
Juice of 2 large lemons
Pure Maine maple syrup to taste

Mix together and chill.

Submitted by Nash Valley Farm
Windham

LESLIE'S AND WALT'S MULLED CIDER

The aroma of this mulled cider simmering on the back burner of the Webbers' kitchen stove is a warm ice-breaker for gathered friends and families. Once sipped, it quickly becomes a sure appetite enticer.

½ gallon Maine apple cider
¼ to ½ cup pure Maine maple syrup (to taste)
2 1-inch sticks cinnamon
1 teaspoon whole cloves
1 teaspoon whole allspice
Lemon or orange slices for garnish

Combine cider, maple syrup, cinnamon, cloves, and allspice. Heat thoroughly and simmer for 20 minutes covered. Do not boil. Remove spices. Garnish with slices of lemon or oranges.

An adaptation of Leslie and Walt's recipe
Friends of Jackson Mountain Farm

MAPLE CREAM SODA

"Have you ever tried a maple cream soda?" asks Val after hours of editing this cookbook. "No? Well, I saw this recipe in the paper the other day. I think you should include it with your maple beverages." She instantly jumps up and readily whips together this refreshing drink. It's a winner!

3 tablespoons pure Maine maple syrup
3 tablespoons cream
Ginger ale or 7-up, chilled
Slightly whip together maple syrup and cream in a tall glass. Add ice and fill with soda.

Submitted by Val Vaughan, Yarmouth

MAPLE CHAI TEA

Harry Schwartz, a former writer of "The Maine Ingredient", a weekly food column in the Portland Press Herald, has willingly shared some of his Maine maple recipes with me. The following is one of them.

This is a hot, soothing drink to sip after exercising in the cold outdoors, during a quiet moment at the end of a busy day, or while relaxing in the evening. In other words, whenever you need soothing.

1 cup hot green tea or tea of choice
½ cup milk or vanilla almond soy milk blend
1 tablespoon pure Maine maple syrup (or to taste)
¼ teaspoon vanilla extract
Dash cinnamon
Dash cloves

Prepare tea. In separate small saucepan heat milk, maple syrup, and vanilla.

Stir tea into milk and then pour mixture into mug. Sprinkle with a bit of cinnamon and cloves over top.

Chef Harry

Submitted by Harry Schwartz
Television personality, author, food columnist

MAPLE COCKTAIL

Eric writes, "The Maine Maple Producers Association hosted the annual meeting of the North American Maple Syrup Council and the International Maple Syrup Institute in the fall of 1999. After the meetings, two tour buses were loaded with maple enthusiasts from across the U.S. and Canada and were headed for a three day tour of Maine's Golden Road; The Tour after the Tour." (The Golden Road to northern Somerset County houses the largest sugarbushes in the state.)

"On several previous occasions our maple syrup-producing friends from Ohio had shared this maple cocktail, but never the recipe. However, after they enjoyed Maine's Tour after the Tour in 1999, the Ohio group surprisingly gave it to me in appreciation of a wonderful experience."

Now Eric shares it with you.

An individual serving

    ¾ ounce (1½ tablespoons) pure Maine maple syrup
    ¾ ounce (1½ tablespoons) dry gin
    1 ounce (2 tablespoons) lemon juice
    1 ounce (2 tablespoons) bourbon

A small party (8 servings)

    ¾ cup pure Maine Maple syrup
    ¾ cup dry gin
    1 cup lemon juice
    1 cup bourbon

Submitted by Eric Ellis
Maine Maple Products, Inc. Madison

KAHLUA

Carolyn Small, a well-known Cumberland citizen, keeps a bottle of homemade kahlua in her refrigerator. She claims it as her comfort thing—a tad of kahlua mixed with milk. "Such a smooth and relaxing drink," she says. "A definite treat—for special occasions or anytime!"

Making maple syrup is a family tradition at the Small's. "Once you've had a taste of real maple syrup," she quips, " you don't want that other stuff." The same is true of her "real" kahlua.

4 cups water
1½ cups white sugar
½ cup granulated Maine maple sugar
4 tablespoons instant coffee (or ¼ cup)
1 cup pure Maine maple syrup-the darker the better
Fifth of vodka
7 teaspoons vanilla extract

Bring water, white sugar, maple sugar and instant coffee to boil, stirring occasionally. Reduce heat; simmer for 30 minutes. Remove from heat and cool completely. Stir in maple syrup, vodka and vanilla extract.

Mix small portions with milk to enjoy.

Submitted by Eric Ellis
Maine Maple Products, Inc. Madison

MAPLE MEAD

The earliest evidence of winemaking dates from about 1000 B.C. in the Middle East, probably in what is now called Turkey. From there, grapevines and winemaking knowledge spread to Egypt, Persia, Greece, and then to Rome. However, the Romans used little of it themselves; their motto—a conquering soldier is a sober soldier. However, their vines and the winemaking process spread throughout southern Europe and into England. The barbarians of northern Europe, who repelled Roman conquest, made their wine from honey, called Mead.

Wine prepared from honey is popular even now, and Mead recipes are still found in winemaking cookbooks. John's recipe was adapted from C.J.J. Berry's, First Steps in Winemaking. He was flipping through the book one day and noticed the Mead recipe, thought about his available resources, and burst out, "Ah, ha! My maple syrup!" And his recipe for Maple Mead was born.

"The finished wine made from Light Amber maple syrup tasted, as winemakers would say, delicate with a hint of maple. On the other hand," he declares, "the wine made from Extra Dark maple syrup was quite strong, probably more suited to the barbarians."

4 pounds pure Maine maple syrup (Light Amber)
Juice from 1 orange
Juice from 1 lemon
3 teaspoons citric acid blend
2 teaspoons yeast nutrient
½ ounce all-purpose wine yeast
 1 gallon water

MAPLE MEAD (continued)

Put maple syrup into water and heat to a boil. Pour into fermentation bucket and cool. Add orange juice, lemon juice, acid blend, and yeast nutrient. Let sit 24 hours and then add yeast and cover. After fermentation is established—two to three days—transfer into glass carboy and fit with airlock. Allow fermentation to complete (no further bubbles), rack (siphon) wine off yeast sediment, and replace in clean carboy fitted with airlock. Wine should be aged for at least a year, but folks with little will power have been known to age it for only an hour.

Makes 1 gallon.

Submitted by John Hodgkins
Jackson Mountain Farm, Temple

IV

CEREALS

Starting the day with a bowl of hot cereal gives you that stick-to-your-ribs energy for the morning. "But," I hear you protest, "hot cereal is bland, boring!"

"Well, doctor it up with a sprinkle of Maine maple sugar or drizzle Maine maple syrup over it," I offer.

"It makes all the difference. I do it every morning." exclaims our friend, Allan, who used to protest, as well.

Also, doll it up with raisins, craisins, dried fruit pieces, fresh apple chunks, fresh berries, a spoonful of your favorite jam, a variety of nuts and seeds. Now you have a bowl of hearty breakfast that's not only delicious and nutritious, but chockfull of interesting flavors and textures! For example, the other morning after I had zapped my oat bran and water mixture in the micro, I added chopped almonds and sliced fresh strawberries. Then I splashed it with a half teaspoon of pure maple syrup and a dribble of skim milk. My! I thought I was eating pudding for breakfast. Try it and our other recipes that follow.

MAPLE-CRANBERRY OATMEAL

"It will give you a bundle of flavor and nutrition as well as energy, plus a more interesting texture," writes Chef Harry.

2 cups water
2¼ cups skim milk or soy milk
2 cups rolled oats
1 cup dried cranberries
1 tablespoon butter
2/3 cup pure Maine maple syrup
1 tablespoon Maine maple sugar or brown sugar
1 teaspoon cinnamon
1 tablespoon orange zest

In 2-quart pan over medium heat, bring water and milk to slow boil and stir in oats and cranberries. Slow boil for 5 minutes. Stir in butter, maple syrup, sugar, cinnamon, and orange zest.

Serves 4.

Chef Harry

Submitted by Harry Schwartz
Television personality, author, food columnist

55

BAKED OATMEAL

Dale, the owner and cook at Magnetic Hill Bed & Breakfast at Moncton, New Brunswick, claims this is the recipe that his guests want to take home. This baked dish adds a healthy and scrumptious dimension to a breakfast or brunch buffet table. The texture is a compromise between the soft and moist cooked oatmeal and the dry crunch of granola. Chopped walnuts or almonds, small chunks of apple, a couple of shakes of cinnamon, add nutrition and interest to the dish. Have some leftover? Heat in microwave with a bit of milk or cream the next morning or freeze for later. Simply halve the recipe for a family meal.

½ cup canola or olive oil
½ cup pure Maine maple syrup
2 eggs
3 cups rolled oats
1¾ teaspoons baking powder
¼ teaspoon baking soda
¼ teaspoon salt
¾ cup milk
Chopped nuts, apples, a couple shakes of cinnamon (optional)

Beat together oil, maple syrup, and eggs. Add to the mixture rolled oats, baking powder, baking soda, salt, and milk and mix. Add nuts, apples, cinnamon, if using. Pour into ovenproof casserole dish (9 x 9 inches). Bake at 350 degrees for 40 to 45 minutes. This is especially delicious served with raisins that have been simmering for approximately 10 minutes. And if you really want to indulge, pour on cream and more pure Maine maple syrup.

Adapted from Dale Luttes' recipe
Magnetic Hill B&B, New Brunswick

SWISS BREAKFAST OATMEAL

*When John and I were in the Swiss Alps with some other hikers
and staying in an old traditional inn, I noticed a serving bowl of
cold, blah-looking mush placed on our buffet table each morning.
I watched my fellow hikers indulging—first the mush, then raisins,
chopped walnuts, pumpkin seeds, flax seeds, homemade berry jam
dabbed in the middle, fresh cream poured over all. "Sundaes?" I
thought. My mind was awhirl with curiosity.*

*"Do you mind if I ask you what you're eating this morning?" I
cautiously ask my new friend, Joan, trying not to be too nosey.
"Oh, that's European muesli. I make a version of it often. It's so
easy for a hurried breakfast and so packed with nutrition. Our
school kids, half awake, pull it from the refrigerator and create
their own dish. You just mix it up the night before. I'll send you the
recipe after we get home—and you should use your maple syrup to
sweeten it."*

*Well, I got up courage and made my own "cereal sundae". I was
hooked, and I feasted on this unbelievable, luscious, fiber-loaded
concoction for the rest of my stay amongst the picture-book scenery
of Swiss peaks.*

1/3 cup old-fashioned oats
1/3 cup milk
1/3 cup shredded apple or crushed pineapple
1 teaspoon lemon juice
Pure Maine maple syrup to taste

Mix together, cover and refrigerate over night. (It will keep 2 to
3 days.) When ready to eat, make your own "cereal sundae".
Indeed, the maple syrup makes it better!

Adapted from Joan Oyama's recipe
Honolulu

HOLIDAY GRANOLA

This Holiday Granola makes a unique gift for neighbors and friends. Just bottle it in a clear glass jar and stick a red bow on the top. They won't be able to resist a taste. Then they'll be sprinkling it on their yogurt, ice cream, puddings, and cereals. They'll love it! Don't forget to save some for your own yogurt!

½ cup canola oil
½ cup pure Maine maple syrup
1 cup light brown sugar
6 cups old-fashioned oats
2 cups chopped walnuts or almonds
1 cup wheat germ
1 cup sweetened, shredded coconut (optional)
1 cup raisins
1 cup sweetened, dried cranberries or cherries

Preheat oven to 350 degrees. Place oven racks in center of oven. Spray two 9 x 12 inch cake tins or two 7 x 11 inch jelly roll pans with cooking oil. In a 1-quart microwave-safe bowl or cooking pot combine oil, maple syrup, and brown sugar. Microwave mixture, uncovered, on high for 3 minutes, or stir constantly on stove top, until sugar starts to melt. Remove from heat and whisk until all lumps disappear. In a larger bowl combine the oats, walnuts, wheat germ, and coconut; toss to mix. Pour syrup mixture over oat mixture and mix well. Spread evenly over pans. Put in oven and bake for 10 minutes. Stir, replace pans, and bake 8 to 10 more minutes, until golden brown. Cool to room temperature. Add half of the raisins and half of the cranberries to each pan and mix well. Store in airtight containers. Makes 14 cups.

Adapted from Beverly Mills' food column,
Portland Press Herald

V

BREADS

Everyone loves home-baked bread. The tantalizing aroma of it baking lifts the spirit—waters the mouth. Bread feeds the soul; it is the staff of life.

Even though the ingredients and the methods of baking have changed over the past two thousand years, bread has remained the mainstay of the human diet. Today it's toasted for breakfast and filled for lunch. At dinner it awes the guests, the perfect complement to any meal.

Who can resist a hot muffin or a slice of eye-catching coffee cake with a cup of steaming tea or coffee while swapping chit-chat with friends?

Home-baked bread, also, makes a welcomed gift any time of year. I remember how my dear grandmother, who lived alone until 96 years young and then lived on to see her 101st birthday, loved to open her gift box I made for her every Christmas. The weeks before the holiday, I individually wrapped and labeled three or four muffins, biscuits, or rolls from the batch I was baking for the family supper and popped them into my freezer. Come Christmas, I would fill her gift box with dozens of her favorite breads and place it under her tree.

For several weeks thereafter, when she hankered for hot bread, she pulled her "bread-box" from her freezer, selected an old favorite, heated it in her toaster-oven, and savored every crumb. Undoubtedly, she was reminiscing about the good old days, when she used to yank a cookie sheet mounded with piping hot biscuits daily from her wood-fired oven to feed her active and growing farm family of eight.

Pure Maine maple syrup not only enhances the flavors of the many whole and healthy grains used for baking breads, but it creates a craving for more. Have fun baking (it is worth the effort) and delight in eating these "wonder" breads. Remember what the old timer says, "It's the maple syrup that makes 'em better!"

WHITE BREAD

Expecting to feed a crowd? Sylvie's recipe is the one, for it makes three loaves. No crowd? After they cool, pop a couple into the freezer. Just wrap each loaf tightly in plastic wrap or aluminum foil, and for extra protection, plastic-bag it. It will keep for two to three months. Or, take a fresh loaf to a shut-in. It will make their day!

1 cup warm water
4 teaspoons sugar
2 yeast cakes (or 2 packages of dry yeast)
2 more cups water
½ cup pure Maine maple syrup
1 cup milk
3 teaspoons salt
1/3 cup butter, melted
10 cups flour (approximately)

Crumble yeast cakes or dry yeast into a bowl with 1 cup of warm water and sugar. Let stand about 10 minutes. Meanwhile combine 2 cups water, maple syrup, milk, salt, and butter. Pour yeast mixture into the second mixture. Gradually add flour until easy to handle. Knead, place in a large greased bowl, and let rise until it doubles in size. Knead again and let rise. Punch down and shape into 3 loaves. Place in greased loaf pans and let rise until doubled in size. Bake at 350 degrees until crust becomes lightly browned and sounds hollow on the bottom when tapped. (Gently tip out of pan to test.) Remove from pans immediately and place on a cooling rack.

Submitted by Sylvie Pare
Dole Pond Maple Products, Quebec

SEVEN-GRAIN BREAD

Ummmm! Does this sound tempting? Coffee, Maine maple syrup, and maple sugar, whole grains! A must try!

1 cup brewed coffee
¾ cup boiling water
½ cup maple syrup
1/3 cup vegetable oil
1 cup old-fashioned 7-grain cereal (or oats)
2/3 cup maple sugar
2 teaspoons salt
2 packages dry yeast dissolved in ¼ cup warm water
2 eggs, slightly beaten
5 ½-6 cups flour

In large mixing bowl combine coffee, boiling water, maple syrup, oil, cereal or oats, maple sugar, and salt. In small bowl add yeast to ¼ cup warm water. Stir until dissolved and add to first mixture. Add eggs and 2 cups flour. Mix. Stir in remaining flour to form soft dough. Turn onto floured surface and knead until smooth and elastic, (6-8 minutes).

Place in greased bowl, turning once to grease. Cover and let rise in warm place until doubled in size. (About one hour). Punch down, turn onto floured surface and cut in half. Shape into 2 loaves and place into loaf pans. Cover and let rise until doubled. (About 30 minutes). Bake at 350 degrees for 40-50 minutes.

Submitted by Kristi Brannen
Spring Break Maple & Honey, Smyrna

WHOLE WHEAT MAINE MAPLE SYRUP BREAD

John writes, "I have this vision of bread, that real bread—what in the seventeenth century some called the staff of life—is soulful and life-giving. But I have not been able, until now, to duplicate my vision.

I have made bread in a kitchen oven, pretty much the Betty Crocker version of traditional white yeast bread. I have made bread in a reflector oven by a blazing riverbank campfire, in a Dutch oven sitting on a bed of hot coals, in a fry pan heated on a hot grill, and wrapped around a stick held over a blaze, but never, before now, have I made bread, or eaten it, that was soulful—bread that I envision monastery monks would eat and then smile.

Below I have arranged a revision of a Betty Crocker bread recipe, one that satisfies my vision of monastery bread. I make it in a kitchen oven for Father's Day or for my birthday when I usually order up something special to eat, like spaghetti—sans Italian bread. (Nothing weakens the pleasure of a good plate of spaghetti like Italian bread.) I am an American. I eat American bread with American spaghetti.

My bread (the monastery version) requires coarse grained whole wheat flour, skim milk, and a generous portion of pure Maine maple syrup. I call it Whole Wheat Maine Maple Syrup Bread. It's so-o-o-o good. It sweetens the disposition of monastery monks, and softens aging.

Try it—"

WHOLE WHEAT MAINE
MAPLE SYRUP BREAD (*continued*)

2 packages yeast (5 teaspoons)
½ cup warm water
¾ cup pure Maine maple syrup
2 teaspoons salt
¼ cup canola oil
1¾ cups skim milk
4 cups whole wheat flour
Variable (1 cup or so) all-purpose flour

Dissolve the yeast in the warm water in a large mixing bowl. Stir in Maine maple syrup, salt, canola oil, milk, and whole wheat flour. Beat with an electric mixer at low speed for ½ minute, continuously keeping sides of bowl scraped. Beat mixture 3 minutes at high speed. Stir in enough all-purpose flour by hand to make dough easy to handle—say a bit stiffer than the consistency of sheet rock compound.

On a lightly floured surface, knead until smooth and elastic (6-8 minutes). Place in a greased bowl and then turn over to expose a greased surface. Cover. Let rise in a warm place for about an hour until an indentation made with a finger will remain. Size of dough should have doubled.

Back on the floured surface again, push the dough flat and cut in half for 8½ x 4½ loaf pans. (If you are using smaller pans, divide in thirds or quarters.) Flatten each half with hands into a rectangle approximately 9 x 18 inches. Fold crosswise into thirds (the second fold will overlap the first). Roll the dough tightly towards you, sealing each turn with thumbs. Push each end downward and fold under. Shape gently to fit loaf pans.

Place loaves in greased loaf pans. Brush lightly with softened butter. Let rise until double—about one hour. Place loaves on rack so that tops of pans are in center of oven. Bake at 375 degrees for about 40 minutes, or sounds hollow when tapped.

Submitted by John Hodgkins
Jackson Mountain Farm, Temple

MEAL-IN-A-LOAF-BREAD

A slice of this bread is not only delish, but it's extra "nutrish". Eat one and you'll crave another, but you'll feel so-o-o healthy! One of my all time favorites!

Also, this bread wrapped in plastic wrap and tied with a colorful ribbon makes a healthy gift for a convalescing friend and a very welcomed present for birthdays and Christmas.

2 cups old-fashioned oats
¼ cup pure Maine maple syrup
¼ cup pure Maine honey
2 teaspoon salt
1 package dry yeast, dissolved in ½ cup water
2 cups milk
1 tablespoon butter
2 cups whole wheat flour
½ cup rye flour
2 to 3 cups unbleached white flour

Combine oats, maple syrup, honey, and salt. Scald milk and add butter. Add to oats mixture. Cool to lukewarm and add dissolved yeast. Mix in whole wheat and rye flours. Then add enough white flour to make soft dough. Knead until smooth. Place in greased bowl and turn to grease all sides of dough. Cover and let rise until doubled. Knead again and shape into loaves—two large ones or 3 to 4 smaller ones (nice for gifts). Bake at 350 degrees until lightly browned and taps hollow on bottom. Remove and cool on rack.

POTATO-MAPLE ROLLS

"Strong men have been known to weep for joy when first biting into one of these," writes Virginia Williams Bentley in her Bentley Farm Cookbook in reference to Gladys Elvinken's potato rolls. Here is Penny's adaptation of Gladys' recipe. Penny says, "These make mouth-watering hamburger rolls and they freeze well. I often make a double batch. They sell well at the Farmers Market, also."

1 cup mashed potato
½ cup lukewarm water
1 cup warm (not hot) potato water, reserved from the
    cooking of the potatoes
2/3 cup pure Maine maple syrup, (Dark or Extra Dark is
    best), at room temperature
2¼ teaspoons dried yeast (one package)
1 cup melted butter
4 eggs, well beaten
2 teaspoons salt
About 6 cups all-purpose flour,
    enough to make soft dough

Combine potato, ½ cup water, potato water, and maple syrup and sprinkle dry yeast over mixture. Let stand about a half hour, until it looks spongy. Stir into above the butter, then eggs, then salt, and last, enough flour to make soft dough (in that order). Let dough rise until double (2-3 hours).
Turn onto floured surface and knead lightly and slightly.

Roll out to 1 inch thickness; cut with biscuit cutter or small soup can. Place on baking sheet about 2 inches apart. Let rise until double (about 1 hour). Bake in preheated 425 degree oven for 10-12 minutes (until golden). Serve hot.

Submitted by Penny Savage
Mitchell and Savage Maple Syrup, Bowdoin

MAPLE BRAN ROLLS

These dark and subtly sweet rolls are an old favorite of mine. They are a scrumptious complement served with any meal, but especially yummy eaten with baked beans, a luncheon salad, or a patio cookout with grilled meat and salads. They are, also, best sellers at the church fair food table. Just wrap in plastic by twos, fours, sixes or by the dozen and watch the packages disappear.

½ cup hot pure Maine maple syrup
½ cup boiling water
½ cup whole bran or oat bran
1/3 cup canola oil
1½ teaspoon salt
2 envelopes dry yeast
½ cup lukewarm water
3 tablespoons powered milk (optional)
2 eggs, beaten
3 ½ to 4 cups unbleached flour

Combine maple syrup, boiling water, bran, oil, and salt and cool until lukewarm. Meanwhile, soften yeast in ½ cup lukewarm water. Add yeast, powdered milk, and eggs to the above cooled mixture. Stir in flour to make soft dough. Knead until smooth. Place in a greased bowl, turn dough in bowl to grease all sides, and let rise until double. Knead again, roll dough to about ½ inch, and shape into rolls (I use a biscuit cutter, then brush with melted butter and fold over). Place, touching, on greased cookie sheet. Cover with waxed paper and rise until double. Remove waxed paper and bake in 400 degree oven 10 to 15 minutes, until golden and hollow sounding when tapped. Brush with butter. Makes 15 to 18 rolls.

Adapted from Beatrice Vaughan's recipe
Maple Cooking

MAPLE WALNUT ROLLS

*For this recipe I must thank my friend, Mary Webber.
Mary is the author of Frugal Family Cookbook, first printed in
1974 and revised several times. (My first copy Mary gave to my
husband, when he served as her guest speaker on her radio show
during maple season.) As I skimmed through it, the maple rolls
caught my eye as a must-try recipe. Well, I have been making these
maple delicacies at Christmas for over 30 years!*

*Over the holidays my family eagerly anticipates the opportunity
to munch down a couple of these maple buns accompanying the
traditional cheese chowder served Christmas Eve or gracing the
table along with John's cheesy omelets and fresh fruit salad for
Christmas breakfast. They simply add elegance in taste and appeal
to any meal!*

*An advantage of this recipe for me is it makes three small batches
(8 buns each) at a time. Serve all three if entertaining a crowd, or
freeze one or two for later. Wrap them in plastic wrap and holiday
ribbon for extremely attractive gifts, or donate them to the church
fair.*

*Another plus: the rolls can be made the day before (up to 24 hours)
and be freshly baked for breakfast. Oh, the tantalizing aroma! The
sleepy heads will stop yawning and rush to the table!*

*Hint: To make the rolling out of dough and clean-up easier, I mark
the dimensions of an 8 x 12 inch rectangle on the back side of
waxed paper with a marker. I then roll the dough out on the floured
topside within the lines. I can easily see what size and shape to roll
the dough.*

MAPLE WALNUT ROLLS *(continued)*

6 cups unbleached flour (approximately)
½ cup white sugar
1½ teaspoon salt
2 envelopes dry yeast
½ cup softened butter
2 cups very hot tap water
2 eggs
1 cup chopped walnuts or pecans
¾ cup packed brown sugar
6 tablespoons pure Maine maple syrup
Melted butter (about 3 tablespoons)

Mix together 2 cups flour, white sugar, salt and yeast. Add softened butter. Gradually add hot water and beat well. Add eggs and ½ cup flour and beat well again. Stir in enough flour to make soft dough. Knead on lightly floured surface until smooth and elastic. Place in greased bowl and turn to grease top of dough. Cover and let rise until double. Meanwhile, combine nuts, brown sugar, and maple syrup.

Punch dough down and divide into thirds. Roll each third into a rectangle 8 x 12 inches. Brush with melted butter and sprinkle with nut mixture. Roll up like a jelly roll and slice into eight slices. Place, cut side up, into a greased 8 or 9 inch cake pan. (If desire, drizzle a bit more maple syrup over the top and sprinkle with a few more nuts. Yum!) Cover and let rise about an hour (until double). Bake at 375 degrees about 20 to 25 minutes.

To bake off the next day: After kneading, cover and let rise only 20 minutes. Punch down, cut into thirds, roll, fill, roll up, slice, and put into greased pans. Brush with oil and cover loosely with plastic wrap. Refrigerate. When ready to bake, let stand at room temperature, while oven heats to 375 degrees and bake 20 to 25 minutes.

JOHNNYCAKE (CORNBREAD)

*This recipe is from one of Aunt Marion's recipe boxes. She was a
long time, enthusiastic supporter of Jackson Mountain Farm in
Temple, which was started over 40 years ago by her three nephews,
John, Brud, and Bill Hodgkins, all from the area at that time.
Every spring she looked forward to delivering the farm's pure
Maine maple syrup to her many colleagues at the University of
Maine in Orono.*

*This is moist cornbread that doesn't crumble until it's in your
mouth! Especially luscious with baked beans, chili, pea or bean
soup, or a luncheon salad. For a breakfast treat add a few raisins
and chopped nuts; and after baked, slice and toast on the griddle.*

1 cup cornmeal
1 cup unbleached flour
¼ teaspoon salt
1 cup sour milk (dissolve 1 tablespoon vinegar in
                regular milk and let sit a few minutes)
1 teaspoon baking soda
1 egg, slightly beaten
4 tablespoons pure Maine maple syrup
2 tablespoons molasses

Combine cornmeal, flour, and salt. Dissolve baking soda in sour
milk and add to dry ingredients along with the egg, maple syrup
and molasses. Stir until moistened and turn into an 8 x 8 inch
greased pan. Bake in 400 degree oven for 15 to 20 minutes,
toothpick is clean when withdrawn.

Adapted from Aunt Marion's recipe.
Jackson Mountain Farm, Temple

BRAN MUFFINS

Luscious and moist! So tasty you won't need to get out the butter or the jam. Eat on the grab, or enjoy with bacon and eggs.

1 cup sour cream
2/3 cup pure Maine maple syrup
3 eggs, well beaten
1 cup flour
1 teaspoon baking power
½ teaspoon baking soda
1 cup All-Bran cereal
½ cup raisins
½ cup chopped nuts

Combine sour cream, maple syrup, and eggs. In a separate bowl mix together flour, baking powder, and baking soda. Add bran, raisins and nuts. Then add liquid ingredients to dry ingredients and mix quickly. Do not beat. Spoon into greased muffin tins. Bake in 350 degree oven for about 15 to 20 minutes.

Submitted by Nash Valley Farm
Windham

Hint: Always serve your muffins piping hot nestled into a cloth napkin lining the breadbasket.

MULTI-GRAIN MAPLE MUFFINS

This recipe comes from Zara's recipe box. Since she and her hubby, Bill, are cancer survivors, she chooses recipes that include nutrient-packed ingredients. These muffins are not only nutritious, but score in taste as well.

¾ cup whole wheat flour
¾ cup yellow cornmeal
½ cup rye flour
2 teaspoons baking powder
¼ teaspoon baking soda
½ teaspoon salt
½ cup rolled oats
1 egg, beaten
1½ cups milk
¼ cup canola oil
¼ cup pure Maine maple syrup

Stir together whole wheat flour, cornmeal, rye flour, baking powder, baking soda, salt, and oats. In another bowl, mix egg, milk, oil, and maple syrup. Then add to dry ingredients and stir to moisten. Fill greased muffin tin and bake in 400 degree oven for 15 to 20 minutes. Makes 14 muffins.

Submitted by Zara Briggs, Yarmouth
Friend of Jackson Mountain Farm

✗ CARROT CORNMEAL MUFFINS

More muffins from Zara's box that also are nutrient-packed, pass the taste test and are naturally sweetened with maple syrup. The yogurt and carrots make for a delightfully moist "little muff", as she calls it.

"I don't understand why my bride goes to all this work to make muffins with maple syrup. I'd just drink it!" raves Bill, Zara's hubby for over fifty years.

1 cup whole wheat flour
1 cup cornmeal
2 teaspoons baking powder
½ teaspoon baking soda
¼ teaspoon salt
3 eggs, beaten
½ cup pure Maine maple syrup
¼ cup canola oil
1 cup plain yogurt
1½ cup grated carrots

Combine flour, cornmeal, baking powder, baking soda, and salt. Stir in eggs, maple syrup, oil and yogurt. Then add carrots. Fill greased muffin tin and bake in 375 degree oven for 15 to 20 minutes.

Submitted by Zara Briggs, Yarmouth
Friend of Jackson Mountain Farm

OLD-FASHIONED MUFFINS

Light and gently mapled treasures to melt in your mouth, or to enhance any ham and egg dish. Dress the tops with finely chopped nuts, if you wish.

2 cups unbleached flour
1 tablespoon baking powder
½ teaspoon baking soda
½ teaspoon salt
1 egg
3 tablespoons canola oil
½ cup pure Maine maple syrup
½ cup milk

In bowl stir together flour, baking powder, baking soda, and salt. In another bowl combine egg, oil, maple syrup and milk. Add liquid ingredients to dry ingredients, mixing until all is moistened. Bake in 400 degree oven for 15 to 20 minutes.

From an old maple advertising flyer

DROP BISCUITS

A delicious maple-sweet bread for breakfast or brunch. Serve them with eggs and bacon. For dessert, spoon sliced strawberries over the biscuit and top with maple syrup and whipped cream. Jocelyn says to put cream and sugar on them.

5 cups flour
1 cup brown sugar
2 teaspoons baking soda
Salt
1 cup shortening
1 cup pure Maine maple syrup
1 cup milk
1 egg

Preheat oven to 375 degrees. Mix flour, sugar, baking soda, and salt together. Cut in shortening. Add maple syrup, milk, and egg. With a spoon, drop dough onto a baking sheet. Bake in oven at 375 degrees for about 15 minutes. Makes 15 to 18 biscuits.

Submitted by Jocelyn Cloutier
Quebec

MAPLE-TOPPED BISCUITS

A traditional recipe baked with a sweet flare; a real breakfast treat!

First make the following topping.

¼ cup pure Maine maple syrup
¼ cup melted butter

Mix the maple syrup and melted butter together. Let set until mixture starts to gel. Meanwhile make the following biscuit dough.

2 cups flour
3 teaspoons baking powder
½ teaspoon salt
¼ cup shortening
¾ cup milk

Mix flour, baking powder, and salt. Cut in shortening until crumbly. Add milk and mix until moistened. Knead lightly on floured surface. Roll to ½ inch thick and cut with a 2 inch round cutter or the end of a soup can. Place biscuits on ungreased cookie sheet. Brush generously with above topping. Bake in oven at 400 degrees for 10 to 12 minutes.Makes 6 to 8 large biscuits.

Submitted by Diane Haulk
Haulk's Maple, Madison

MAPLE NUT SCONES

"We make it ourselves!" Val, a former backyard producer, and her family liked to boast when their out-of-state relatives and friends visited. "Every spring we'd tap the two big maples in the backyard. We'd make about 8 quarts a year. Cindy, our daughter, remembers it took a long, long time for the sap to reach syrup. And I will never forget boiling a batch to burnt sugar while I chatted on the phone! But, I fondly remember how the house—fortunately furnished with minimum wallpaper—filled with a sweet fog as the season's sap simmered on the back burner of the kitchen stove for hours and hours! Our mouths would water with anticipation—and when friends came for coffee, we treated them with these sure-to-please scones."

2 cups flour
1 tablespoon baking powder
¼ teaspoon baking soda
¼ teaspoon salt
¼ cup cold butter
½ cup finely chopped pecans
1/3 cup cream
¼ cup pure Maine maple syrup
1 whole egg
1 egg yolk

Preheat oven to 400 degrees. Stir together flour, baking powder, baking soda, and salt. Cut in butter to resemble coarse crumbs. Add pecans. Combine cream, maple syrup, and whole egg and stir into dry ingredients, just enough to hold dough together. Knead 30 seconds. Pat or roll dough to a ½ inch thick circle and cut into wedges. Mix egg yolk with 1 tablespoon water and brush tops of scones with it. Place scones one inch apart on buttered cookie sheet, and bake for 15 minutes or until brown.

Submitted by Val Vaughan
Yarmouth

MAPLE WALNUT AND OATMEAL SCONES

Edwina writes, "Friends and relatives enjoy these delicious scones." And they do sound delicious!

3 cups flour
4 teaspoons baking powder
¾ teaspoon salt
1/3 cup brown sugar, packed
¼ teaspoon cinnamon
¾ cup unsalted butter
½ cup chopped walnuts
½ cup oats
1/3 cup pure Maine maple syrup
1 teaspoon vanilla extract
2/3 cup milk or light cream
About 3 tablespoons butter, melted
¼ cup brown sugar, packed
¼ cup pure Maine maple syrup

Preheat oven to 425 degrees. Grease baking sheet. Combine flour, baking powder, salt, 1/3 cup brown sugar, and cinnamon. Cut in ¾ cup butter until a sandy texture. Add walnuts and oats. Make a well in the center and add 1/3 cup maple syrup, vanilla, and most of milk or cream. Stir with fork to make soft dough. Briefly knead to make a cohesive mass, adding a bit more milk, if needed (if dough is too dry). Shape into two rounds about ¾ inch thick. Cut into wedges and place on baking sheet. Brush each with melted butter. Then combine ¼ cup brown sugar and ¼ cup maple syrup and drizzle over scones. Bake about 15 minutes. Makes 12 to 16 servings.

Submitted by Edwina Hardy
Mountain Maple, Rumford

ZUCCHINI BREAD

So you have an abundant crop of garden zucchini? After trying this maple zucchini bread recipe, you'll hanker for it every summer. But don't wait until next summer, bake some extra loaves now for the freezer, or freeze your grated zucchini and enjoy freshly baked maple zucchini bread mid-winter, and dream summer.

¾ cup sugar
2 teaspoons vanilla extract
½ cup canola oil
3 eggs
1½ cups pure Maine maple syrup
2 cups grated zucchini
½ cup milk
2 ½ cups unbleached flour
2 teaspoons baking soda
1½ teaspoons baking powder
¾ teaspoon salt
1 teaspoon cinnamon
½ cup chopped nuts

Preheat oven to 350 degrees. Cream sugar, vanilla, oil, and eggs until fluffy. Mix in maple syrup, zucchini, and milk. Combine flour, baking soda, baking powder, salt, and cinnamon; and add to wet ingredients. Mix thoroughly. Stir in nuts. Pour into 2 greased loaf pans lined with waxed paper, 4 small loaf pans, or a large tube pan. Choose Option 1 or Option 2 printed on the next page and proceed with directions.

OPTION 1: A Crumb Topping—to sprinkle on top of bread just before you pop it into the oven. Some of the topping will sink into the bread creating sweet wells of thick, buttery maple. Oh, so delish!

ZUCCHINI BREAD (continued)

½ cup brown sugar
2 tablespoons butter
2 tablespoons pure Maine maple syrup
3 tablespoons flour

Cut butter into brown sugar. Mix in maple syrup and flour.
Sprinkle on top of bread dough and bake for 40 to 50 minutes,
or until tested done with toothpick. Remove from pans and peel
off waxed paper lining. Cool on rack.

*OPTION 2: Bake bread without topping for about 40 to 50
minutes. Remove from pans, peel off lining, and cool on rack.
When cooled, drizzle with maple icing if desired.*

Maple Icing

1 cup confectioners' sugar
Pure Maine maple syrup (2 to 3 tablespoons)

Mix enough maple syrup into the sugar to create a thick drizzle.
Zigzag icing as it sheds from spoon across the top of bread to
create a decorative look.

BLUEBERRY WALNUT BREAD

A healthy, moist, and delish sweet bread to offer with tea or coffee, or to serve for dessert with a bowl of fresh fruit.

2 eggs
1 cup sour cream
½ cup pure Maine maple syrup
½ cup sugar
1 teaspoon vanilla extract
½ cup wheat bran or bran cereal
1½ cups unbleached flour
½ teaspoon salt
1 teaspoon baking soda
1 cup fresh or frozen Maine blueberries
1 cup chopped walnuts
2 tablespoons pure Maine maple sugar or cinnamon sugar
    (optional)

Preheat oven to 350 degrees. In mixing bowl beat eggs, sour cream, maple syrup, sugar and vanilla. Stir in bran. In separate bowl sift together flour, salt, and baking soda. Add flour mixture to wet ingredients and stir gently until just moistened. Stir in blueberries and walnuts. Pour into greased loaf pan and sprinkle with maple sugar or cinnamon sugar, if desire. Bake 40 to 50 minutes, or until tests done. Makes one standard-sized loaf or two smaller ones.

RHUBARB COFFEE CAKE

This maple and rhubarb coffee cake will impress your guests at breakfast, at coffee, or at dessert when garnished with a dollop of maple whipped cream. The sour cream keeps it moist and the maple blended with rhubarb and cinnamon creates a flavor to savor.

½ cup pure Maine maple syrup
½ cup brown sugar
½ cup butter
1 egg
2 cups unbleached flour
1 teaspoon baking soda
½ teaspoon salt
2/3 cup sour cream
1½ cups to 2 ½ cups cut rhubarb (about ½ inch pieces)
      coated with 1 tablespoon maple syrup

Preheat oven to 350 degrees. Cream maple syrup, brown sugar, butter, and egg. Mix flour, baking soda, and salt. Add to creamed mixture alternately with sour cream. Stir in rhubarb. Turn into a greased 9 x 13 inch pan and sprinkle with topping below. Bake for 30 or 40 minutes.

Topping:

 ½ cup brown sugar
2 tablespoons butter
2 tablespoons pure Maine maple syrup
3 tablespoons flour
¼ teaspoon cinnamon
½ cup chopped walnuts

Cut butter into brown sugar. Add maple syrup, flour, cinnamon, and nuts.

VI

MEAT, FISH, AND POULTRY

"Meat is like the star of the show…the center around which the rest of the meal revolves. All other foods are chosen on the basis of how well they go with the meat selected. Meat is also the most expensive item in our food budget… which makes it doubly important that we present this star performer to the best advantage."

Betty Crocker
Betty Crocker's Picture Cookbook

Use pure Maine maple syrup to show off star-performing meat, fish, or poultry to its best advantage? Definitely! Maine maple makes the difference. But, go light. Add as you would a spice, like garlic or basil, not as a sugar. The syrup enhances and seals the flavor as it caramelizes; it also thickens and adds essence to the juices as it slowly cooks.

A bonus! The subtle sweetness of the maple bouquet will permeate the kitchen. It will lift your spirit! Shortly after arrival, dinner guests will certainly ask, "Oh, what's cooking?"

Not expecting guests, just family? Revel in the tantalizing aroma as you prepare the rest of the meal and imagine the first bite. Hope for leftovers or what my friend, Ruth, calls "a second preparation."

Also, in our "Toppings, Glazes, Sauces, and Spreads" section, you will find more recipes and ideas for meat accompaniments and glazes. They will add the final touch to a scrumptious meal.

MEAT RUB

A maple rub; "great on baby back ribs," writes Kristi. "It's quick and tasty."

2 tablespoons butcher black pepper
1 tablespoon Spanish paprika
1-2 tablespoons pure Maine maple sugar
1 tablespoon kosher salt

Coat both sides of meat (pork chops, chicken pieces, ribs) with meat rub and place in oven or on grill to cook. (If baking baby back ribs, bake at 200 degrees for 5 to 6 hours.)

Submitted by Kristi Brannen
Spring Break Maple and Honey, Smyrna

MARVELOUS MARINATED LONDON BROIL STEAK

Get out the grill! This marinade transforms the so-so cut of steak into the marvelous cut of steak.

2 pounds London Broil steak
¼ cup pure Maine maple syrup
2 tablespoons canola oil
3 tablespoons Worcestershire sauce
1 tablespoon soy sauce
Juice of 1 lime
2 teaspoons bottled minced garlic
1 teaspoon onion powder (or to taste)

Whisk together all ingredients. Put meat into a gallon-sized zip top plastic bag. Pour marinade over meat. Seal bag and turn several times to cover meat with marinade. Refrigerate 8-24 hours turning bag at least once. Discard marinade when ready to grill.

MAPLE-JALEPENO BABY BACK RIBS

These baby back ribs, treated with a spicy rub, grilled, and brushed with a sweet and sour maple glaze; make a perfect summertime meal served with a favorite salad and homemade bread.

This recipe comes to us from Jody Haynes, daughter of Ron Haynes, a Maine maple producer from Madison. Recently, she has been a chef/ food connoisseur in Manhattan. However, presently she is practicing her culinary arts on the west coast.

3 racks of baby back ribs
3 cloves of garlic, crushed to paste
1½ teaspoons black pepper
2 tablespoons coriander
1 tablespoon salt
400 ml pure Maine maple syrup (1 2/3 cups)
2 jalapeno, finely minced
120 ml white wine vinegar (1/2 cup)

Combine garlic paste, black pepper, coriander, and salt with mortar and pestle to create a smooth paste. Rub mixture onto rack of ribs and grill on low flame for an hour, turning a few times.

Combine maple syrup, jalapeno, and vinegar with a whisk. Add salt and pepper to taste. During the last 15 minutes of cooking, brush maple glaze onto ribs, one side at a time, turning and brushing every 3 to 5 minutes until caramelized.

Submitted by Jody Haynes

MAPLE-GLAZED PORK TENDERLOIN

Barbara Smith was the #1 candy maker in the state of Maine for many years. However, on occasion she set aside some of the company's syrup and treated her family to this maple-glazed pork tenderloin.

"This recipe makes a good family dinner. Any grade of syrup will do just fine," Barbara shared.

2 ½ pounds pork tenderloin
¾ cup pure Maine maple syrup
1 tablespoon orange juice concentrate
2 tablespoons barbeque sauce
2 tablespoons soy sauce
1 tablespoon Dijon mustard
1 tablespoon Worcestershire sauce
1 tablespoon curry powder
1 garlic clove, pressed or minced
1 teaspoon toasted sesame seeds (optional)

Preheat oven to 350 degrees. Place pork in 11 x 7 inch baking dish. Combine all other ingredients, except sesame seeds, and pour over pork. Bake, uncovered, for 30 minutes to one hour. Remove from oven and allow to stand 10 minutes before slicing into 1/4 inch slices. To serve, place slices onto plates and spoon sauce over meat. Sprinkle with sesame seeds.

Submitted by Barbara Smith
Smith's Maple Products, Skowhegan

MAPLE-MUSTARD PORK TENDERLOIN

A pork tenderloin glazed with maple, mustard and rosemary and served with caramelized apples. "This pork is awesome!" exclaims Penny Savage, a friend of Pip's.

2½ pounds pork tenderloins
Cooking spray
¼ cup Dijon mustard
6 tablespoons pure Maine maple syrup, divided
1 teaspoon rosemary
½ teaspoon salt
¼ teaspoon black pepper
4 medium Granny Smith apples,
    each peeled and cut into 16 wedges

Preheat oven to 425 degrees. Trim fat from pork. Place pork on broiler pan coated with cooking spray. Combine mustard, 2 tablespoons of maple syrup, rosemary, salt and pepper in small bowl; brush over pork. Insert meat thermometer into thickest part of meat. Bake for 25 minutes or until thermometer reads 160 degrees (slightly pink). While pork is baking, heat a nonstick skillet over medium-high heat until hot. Add apples, and sauté 5 minutes, or until apples are lightly browned. Reduce heat to low and add 4 tablespoons of maple syrup. Simmer 10 minutes, until apples are tender, stirring occasionally. Cut pork crosswise into slices; spoon apples over pork. Makes 4 servings.

Submitted by Pip Marrotte, Westbrook
Friend of Mitchell and Savage Maple Syrup

MAPLE PULLED PORK

Another scrumptious "Chef Harry" recipe. It blends a variety of delicious sweet and sour flavors. It is also a convenient make-ahead dish. Just store in refrigerator for a day or two. Serve over buns, sliced in half crosswise.

4-pound pork butt or shoulder, cut in half
2 bay leaves
2 cans beer, or 4 cups apple cider or apple juice
4 slices uncooked bacon, chopped
1 onion, minced
3 cloves fresh garlic, minced
3 cups tomato sauce
½ cup cider vinegar
½ cup brown sugar
2/3 cup pure Maine maple syrup (to taste)
Salt and pepper to taste

Place meat, bay leaves, and beer or apple juice or cider in Dutch oven and slow-cook tightly covered for 4 to 6 hours or until it starts to fall apart. Drain and trim meat. Pull the meat apart and chop it to desired texture.

In a 4 to 6 quart heavy saucepan cook bacon over medium-high heat for 7 minutes and add onion. Sauté until tender. Add garlic to pan and sauté for another 2 minutes. Lower heat to medium-low and stir in tomato sauce, vinegar, brown sugar, and maple syrup. Bring to simmer and cook gently, stirring frequently for 5 minutes. Season to taste with salt and pepper. Adjust the syrup or sugar to taste, also. Add meat to sauce and stir until combined. Cook until meat is reheated.

Chef Harry

Submitted by Harry Schwartz
Television personality, author, food columnist

MAPLE SPARE RIBS

Jim Crocker, a local television personality, used this recipe to create a simple, savory meat on The Maine Dish, his WB51-TV cooking show, one sugaring season to promote pure Maine maple syrup. Needless to say, it was a big hit!

3 pounds pork spare ribs (pork chops work, also)
2½ tablespoons chili sauce (or steak sauce)
2 tablespoons chopped onions
1½ cups pure Maine maple syrup
2 teaspoons salt (or to taste)
½ teaspoon dry mustard
¼ teaspoon chili powder (optional)
1/8 teaspoon black pepper

Simmer spare ribs in salted water for 30 minutes. Drain. Place in 9 x 13 inch baking dish. Combine remaining ingredients and pour over ribs. Bake at 375 degrees for 30 minutes, basting frequently until done. The sauce will be thick and the ribs glazed.

GRILLED HAM

Grilling a ham for dinner? Brush with pure Maine maple syrup the last few minutes of grilling.

BOILED HAM

"You know, ever since we had Easter dinner at your home, I always boil my hams first in maple syrup, cloves, and water. What a difference!" quips Sandi, a guest at our Easter dinner table a couple of years ago.

I always boil ham a day or two before I want to serve it as my meal "star performer". It reduces the sodium content and adds moisture to the meat. I enhance the flavor by adding about 1/3 cup pure Maine maple syrup and ½ teaspoon (give or take) ground cloves per 5 pounds of ham to the boiling water. I simmer it on top of stove for a couple of hours. After it has cooled, I reserve some of the broth for a favorite soup—split pea, legume, black bean, ham and cauliflower—and store the ham in the refrigerator or freeze it until ready to use.

Convenient to have on hand for those dog days of summer. Thaw and serve cold slices with pineapple and a drizzle of maple syrup. Or heat in microwave for a warmed meat.

Or serve with chunky, maple sweetened Apple Sauce, one of the cranberry sauces or chunk for the Cabbage and Apples dish. See index for recipes.

BAKED HAM

To glaze ham while baking use ½ cup pure Maine maple syrup per 5 pound ham. Baste periodically throughout the baking process. Mix syrup with pineapple juice, if desired.

BROILED MAPLE-MUSTARD SALMON

Maple pairs with salmon, like cheese with apple pie!

Here's a heart-healthy dish with a versatile sauce that can be used to baste tuna or chicken, as well as salmon under the broiler or on the grill.

¾ pound fresh salmon fillet
1 tablespoon Dijon mustard
2 tablespoons pure Maine maple syrup
½ teaspoon lemon juice
White pepper and salt to taste
1 teaspoon melted butter

Preheat broiler. Whisk mustard, maple syrup, lemon juice, pepper and salt to taste. Coat broiler pan with oil spray and put fillet on pan. Brush with butter, then sauce and place under broiler. Broil with oven door partially open for about 5 minutes; fish looks pink. Turn over and brush the other side of fish and continue broiling and brushing until fish flakes (not long, keep watch). Serves 2.

Submitted by Michael Smith
Maine Maple Producer, Winthrop

92

MAPLE TERIYAKI SALMON

A few years ago Christmas Day came on Sunday. I needed a special dish for dinner that could be easily prepared ahead and baked quickly upon returning from church. This maple teriyaki salmon, baked in the oven with potatoes, was the perfect answer. Even the grandkids had seconds. Our son, Jack, and daughter-in-law, Victoria, wow their guests every time they serve it at their downtown-Boston home.

This fish is also delicious grilled or broiled. The maple marinade forms a sweet crust on the fish and traps the juices as it caramelizes.

Have some salmon left over? Serve Salmon Salad (recipe found in "Salads" section) for lunch the next day or freeze for next week.

1/3 cup pure Maine maple syrup
1/3 cup apple cider, apple juice, or white wine
3 tablespoons soy sauce
½ small onion, minced
½ teaspoon garlic powder
Black pepper
2 pounds fresh salmon fillet, cut into serving sizes

Whisk together maple syrup, cider, soy sauce, onion, garlic, and pepper to taste. Pour mixture into a zip plastic bag, add salmon pieces and marinate in refrigerator for 1 to 3 hours. A half hour before baking, remove salmon from marinade and let sit at room temperature. Bake in 400 degree oven for about 15 to 20 minutes or until it flakes.

Submitted by Victoria and Jack Hodgkins
Jackson Mountain Farm

MAPLE-GLAZED SALMON

Chef Harry offers a delectable combo of flavors—garlic, ginger, maple, soy sauce, pineapple and olive oil—to baste a grilling salmon. A must try!

2 tablespoons minced garlic
2 tablespoons minced ginger
1/3 cup pure Maine maple syrup
1/3 cup lite soy sauce
1 cup pineapple juice
2 tablespoons canola or extra virgin olive oil
1 piece salmon side fillet, skin on (24 to 30 ounces)
½ cup brown sugar

Whisk together garlic, ginger, maple syrup, soy sauce, pineapple juice and oil. Pour over fish and let stand 20 minutes.

Grill fish, flesh side down first, covered, over medium-hot nonstick grill about 5 minutes. Turn and sprinkle with brown sugar. Grill until done, about 6 to 10 minutes, depending on thickness of salmon. Fish should be pink and flaky. Drizzle more maple syrup over fish just before removing, if desired. Serves 4.

Chef Harry

Submitted by Harry Schwartz
Television personality, author, food columnist

BAKED HADDOCK

This is an adaptation of a winning recipe from a Taste of Maine cooking contest. It is very easy to prepare; the maple enhances.

¾ to 1 pound fresh haddock, cod, or sole
½ cup sour cream
1 teaspoon lemon juice
Salt to taste
4 teaspoons pure Maine maple syrup
½ cup bread crumbs

Preheat oven to 425 degrees. Arrange fish in greased baking dish. Mix sour cream, lemon juice, salt, maple syrup, and bread crumbs and spread over fish. Bake about 30 minutes, fish flakes.

GRILLED CHICKEN WINGS

"Even the kids enjoy eating these!" writes Bob, father of four.

½ onion, chopped fine
1 clove garlic (small-medium), chopped fine
1 tablespoon vegetable oil
½ cup pure Maine maple syrup
½ cup ketchup
1½ to 2 ounces bourbon
1 to 2 teaspoons hot pepper sauce (optional)
½ cup mayonnaise
2½ to 3 pounds chicken wings (or other parts or chicken)

Brown onion and garlic in pan with oil. Add maple syrup, ketchup, and bourbon. Boil 5 minutes. Remove from heat; whisk in pepper sauce and mayonnaise. Slowly grill chicken about 35 minutes, turn once, glaze often. A sweet, delicious glaze.

Submitted by Bob Stephens
Jackson Mountain Farm

MAPLE AND GINGER CHICKEN

Lisanne glazes her chicken with an interesting twist of flavors—maple, fresh ginger, garlic, vinegar, and soy sauce. Sounds delicious. She suggests serving the chicken with mashed potatoes and string beans.

1¼ pounds chicken breast, cut into strips
2 teaspoons vegetable oil
1/3 cup flour
½ cup pure Maine maple syrup or sugar
2 tablespoons cider vinegar
2 tablespoons soy sauce
2 tablespoons sherry (optional)
2 teaspoons fresh ground ginger
2 ground cloves of garlic
½ teaspoon pepper

Preheat oven to 325 degrees. Heat oil in skillet. Coat chicken pieces with flour. Cook chicken in skillet about 5 minutes, until brown on all sides. Transfer pieces to baking dish. Whisk together maple syrup, vinegar, soy sauce, sherry, ginger, garlic, and pepper. Pour over chicken and bake about 10 minutes, or until meat is done.

Submitted by Lisanne Lapointe & Germain Audet
Quebec

PEACHY MAPLE CHICKEN

A tasty combination of fruity flavors accented with pure Maine maple syrup, creates a peach of a dish. A favorite from the South. Serve over rice.

6 skinless, boneless chicken breasts
½ cup flour
Salt and pepper to taste
2 tablespoons butter
2 tablespoons cooking oil
1½ cups orange juice
2 tablespoons vinegar
2 tablespoons pure Maine maple syrup
1 teaspoon basil
½ teaspoon nutmeg
1 can (16 ounces) peach halves, drained

Preheat oven to 375 degrees. Put flour, salt, and pepper into plastic bag and shake. Add chicken pieces and shake until well coated. Melt butter with oil in skillet and brown chicken pieces. Then place it into a greased baking dish. Whisk orange juice with vinegar, maple syrup, basil, and nutmeg. Pour over chicken. Cover and bake until chicken is tender (about 1 hour), basting often. Then add peach halves amongst the chicken, baste, and bake, uncovered, for about 15 minutes longer to thicken juices.

Serves 6.

97

ORANGE THYME CHICKEN BREASTS

Low on time, high on taste? This is the recipe. Prepare in the morning and refrigerate during the day. The marinade can even be made a day or two ahead and kept in the refrigerator. The pure Maine maple syrup and orange juice caramelize to lightly crust the chicken as it bakes and the thyme gives it zip. Share the oven with potato, squash, or sweet potato to conserve on energy.

4 skinless, boneless chicken breasts
½ cup fresh orange juice (Minneola juice is great, too)
2 tablespoons olive oil
2 tablespoons pure Maine maple syrup
1 tablespoon fresh thyme leaves, or powder to taste
Salt and pepper to taste

Whisk together marinade (orange juice, olive oil, maple syrup, thyme, salt and pepper). Pour into baking dish or zip plastic bag. Add chicken and coat well. Cover or zip and refrigerate several hours. Preheat oven to 350 degrees when ready to bake. Place baking dish in heated oven and bake, covered. Baste occasionally until cooked (about 30 minutes).

MAINE MAPLE CIDER CHICKEN

One evening after dining at One Stanley Avenue in Kingfield, my friend Sandi courageously asked Chef Dan for the recipe of her favorite meal, Maine Maple Cider Chicken. He generously gave her a copy, and later readily gave me permission to print it in this book. Chef Dan, also owner of the restaurant, combines pure Maine maple syrup with Maine apples and Maine apple cider to transform ordinary chicken into extraordinary chicken.

¼ cup pure Maine maple syrup
¼ pound sweet butter
1½ cup apple cider
1/3 cup cider vinegar

MAINE MAPLE CIDER CHICKEN
(continued)

1 teaspoon salt
2 tablespoons cornstarch
4 whole chicken breasts, boned and skinned
2 eggs
6 tablespoons clarified butter
1 Granny Smith or Cortland apple

1. Clarified Butter—Place ½ cup butter in a 2-cup glass measuring cup and micro-wave on high for 2 minutes (until boiling) or gradually heat in pan on stove top. The clear layer on top is the clarified butter.

2. Sauce: Mix maple syrup, sweet butter, ½ cup apple cider, vinegar, and salt in saucepan over medium heat until butter is melted. Dilute cornstarch in a little cold water. Stir into mixture to thicken. Set aside on warm heat.

3. Apple-slice topping: Peel and core apple, and cut into thin slices. Bring 1 cup apple cider to a boil over medium heat in a small saucepan. Remove from heat and place apple slices in hot cider. Let stand for 15 minutes. Drain and set aside.

4. Chicken: Pound breasts to an even thinness. Beat eggs briefly to make egg wash. Dip each breast, one at a time, into egg wash. Remove and shake off excess egg. Then dredge breasts in flour. In a large skillet sauté pieces in clarified butter until golden brown and cooked through.

5. Serving: Place chicken breasts on hot platter and top with poached apple slices. Top the chicken with hot maple cider sauce.

Recipe created by Dan Davis,
Chef and owner of One Stanley Avenue

Submitted by Sandi Hudon, Carrabassett Valley and Bristol, CN
Friend of Jackson Mountain Farm

ROASTED CHICKEN AND VEGETABLES

*A fall or winter afternoon is a perfect time to warm the kitchen
while roasting chicken with a medley of winter veggies and a touch
of Maine maple syrup. The mouth will water as the tantalizing
aroma escapes the oven! The crispy, golden chicken centered
amongst the circled vegetables on your favorite platter makes a
very attractive and irresistible meal.*

1 roasting chicken (6 to 7 pounds)
   or 6 large chicken breasts
2 tablespoons butter, melted
Salt and pepper to taste
4 carrots, peeled and cut into 3 inch chunks
4 parsnips, peeled and cut into 3 inch chunks
4 stalks celery, cut into 3 inch chunks
4 potatoes, peeled and cut into 3 inch chunks
4 onions, peeled and quartered
   (may substitute winter squash or sweet potato
   for any of above veggies)
½ teaspoon rosemary
1/3 to ½ cup pure Maine maple syrup

Preheat oven to 400 degrees. Brush chicken with melted butter.
Spread vegetables evenly over bottom of roasting pan. Place
chicken on top of veggies and sprinkle with salt, pepper, and
rosemary. Put pan into oven with the rack on the lowest level.
Baste with maple syrup every 10 minutes. When you run out
of maple syrup, continue to baste with pan juices. Roast until
chicken is golden, crisp, and tender for about 1½ to 2 hours.
(Check for doneness with meat thermometer.)

Submitted by Penny Savage
Mitchell and Savage Maple Syrup, Bowdoin

SWEET AND SOUR CHICKEN

A quick and easy meal that is certain to please everyone around the supper table. The sweet maple softens the sharp edge of the vinegar as it delicately flavors the chicken and vegetables. Serve over brown rice or noodles and sprinkle with toasted almonds for a company flare. Round out the meal with a green salad and a dinner roll.

¼ cup pure Maine maple syrup (Medium or Dark)
2 tablespoons cornstarch or ¼ cup flour
½ teaspoon salt
½ cup juice, drained from canned pineapple
¼ cup apple juice
¼ cup cider vinegar
1 tablespoon soy sauce
3 cups cooked and chunked chicken
¼ cup chopped red pepper
¼ cup sliced mushrooms, canned or fresh
¼ cup chopped onion
1 cup pineapple chunks
½ cup thinly sliced celery
2 cups cooked brown rice
¼ cup slivered toasted almonds (optional)

Whisk together maple syrup, cornstarch, and salt in small bowl. Combine pineapple juice, apple juice, vinegar, soy sauce, and maple mixture in a large saucepan. Bring to boil over medium-high heat; reduce heat to low and cook until thickened, stirring occasionally. Remove from heat and add chicken, red pepper, mushrooms, onion, celery, and pineapple. Cook over medium heat for 8 to 10 minutes, stirring often. Enjoy! Serves 4 to 6.

This freezes well, also.

MAPLE-GLAZED CHICKEN AND RICE

A unique combo of flavors and textures from the maple, nuts, raisins and cinnamon baked with the chicken makes this dish an elegant treat for those gathered at the table. Besides, it is quick and easy to prepare.

1 package (6 ounces) of seasoned rice
1½ cups water
2 large chicken breasts, skinless and boneless
      (about 1 pound)
3 tablespoons pure Maine maple syrup
½ cup chopped walnuts
½ teaspoon ground cinnamon
½ cup raisins

Preheat oven to 350 degrees. Mix uncooked rice, seasoning packet, and water in 8-inch square baking dish. Place chicken breasts on top of rice and drizzle with maple syrup. Sprinkle with cinnamon, walnuts, and raisins. Cover and bake about 45 minutes or until rice is tender and chicken no longer pink in center. Yummy! Serves 3 or 4.

Adapted from *Betty Crocker's Cookbook*

Variation:

4 large skinless chicken thighs (about 1½ pounds)
2 small sweet potatoes, peeled and chunked to 1-inch cubes
1 small onion, cut into 1-inch pieces
8 ounces carrots or parsnips, peeled and cut into 1-inch pieces
¼ cup pure Maine maple syrup
Salt and pepper to taste

Toss all together, place on rice, and bake as above, stirring and turning once.

CHICKEN STIR-FRY

*Just add a tablespoon of pure Maine maple syrup to a
Cantonese stir-fry and you have a Maine maple stir-fry.
And the maple makes it better. A family favorite for years.*

1½ tablespoons soy sauce
2 teaspoons cornstarch
1 tablespoon pure Maine maple syrup
1 teaspoon chicken broth or sherry
1/8 teaspoon garlic powder
2 chicken breasts, skinless and boneless (about 1 pound),
    sliced into strips
2 tablespoons canola or olive oil
½ cup chopped onion
1 cup sliced celery
4 cups fresh vegetables cut to bite size
    (I like carrots, broccoli, mushrooms, pea pods,
    bean sprouts: or when I'm in a hurry, I dump in a bag
    of frozen mixed veggies).
1 teaspoon ground ginger, or 1 tablespoon fresh (to taste)
¼ cup chicken broth

Whisk together soy sauce, cornstarch, maple syrup, one
teaspoon chicken broth or sherry, and garlic powder. Pour
over chicken strips and marinate ½ hour. Meanwhile, prepare
vegetables. Heat oil in wok or skillet; stir-fry chicken and onions
for 5 minutes. Add vegetables of your choice, plus ginger and
stir-fry for 10 minutes. Add broth; cover and heat 2 minutes.
Serve over brown rice. Especially delicious with Fresh Citrus
Salad (recipe found in "Salads" section) and homemade dinner
rolls. Serves 4.

VII

MAIN DISHES
BAKED BEANS, CHILI, SOUPS, PASTA

For a homey meal with family, a hearty lunch with friends, a Sunday night supper, or to add variety to the weekly menu, prepare a one-pot meal. Make it a day or two ahead, which gives the flavors in the dish time to season, and heat at the last minute for convenience.

Don't forget to add the pure Maine maple syrup. It adds character all of its own to dishes and soups. Be creative and revitalize your old recipes with a touch of maple sweetness. You want to enhance and blend the flavors; however, be careful not to drown them. You want only a hint.

Serve with a crisp salad and a slice of homemade bread or a hot quick bread and you have an appealing, well-balanced, and tasty meal to feed the hungries. It's the maple that makes 'em better.

BOSTON BAKED BEANS

Reading this recipe sends me on a nostalgia trip back to my childhood days. Every Saturday morning—yes, every Saturday morning—I'd awake to baked bean aroma gently floating throughout the old farmhouse, the walls no barrier. My brothers and I wished the day away as we eagerly waited with watering mouths for our traditional plate of Saturday night baked beans served with Mom's fluffy biscuits or cornbread and cabbage salad or applesauce. What a treat!

But get this! Not only did we have them every Saturday night, but every Sunday morning with toast. Monday and Tuesday it was cold bean sandwiches in the school lunchboxes; and finally, Wednesday supper saw the last bean swallowed for the week! Imagine! And in three more days the cycle would start all over again.

After all that, you'd think I'd hate the thought of beans, but I still love them, especially if they are baked with pure Maine maple syrup.

I understand the English, who grew-up with beans, bacon and pottage, brought their recipes with them on their first voyage to what is now New England. But once here, they learned the Natives had been growing a different variety of bean for centuries and probably baking them in earthen pots and sweetening them with maple sugar. This new and different bean, the pea bean, soon became the bean of choice for the settlers. Soon after the English settled, baked beans became their traditional Saturday night supper. Being an easy and economical meal, beans shared the fired oven with other baked goods—breads, pies, puddings—for the upcoming week. And the leftover beans were served for breakfast Sunday mornings since Boston's Puritan women were forbidden to cook on the Sabbath.

I'm amazed that I am the 13th generation to carry on that tradition! Why? I guess because my mother did, and her mother and her mother and her mother and her mother ...

And now for Penny's and Gwen's favorite recipe!

BOSTON BAKED BEANS (continued)

(Included are conflicting amounts of sweetening. If you prefer a not-so-sweet bean dish, go with the lesser amount.)

4 cups or 2 pounds of dry beans (Jacob's Cattle, Yellow Eye, or Soldier) picked over and washed
1 medium onion, peeled
½ pound salt pork, cut into small pieces
2 teaspoons salt, or to taste
½ to 1 teaspoon dry mustard
½ teaspoon dry ginger
¼ cup molasses or ½ cup brown sugar
¾ to 2 cups pure Maine maple syrup, (Dark or Extra Dark)

Soak beans in water 2 inches covering, overnight. Parboil by bringing kettle to boiling, reduce heat to a simmer. Cook on low heat until beans peel when blown on after dipping a few out with a spoon. Drain beans, reserving water. Place onion, then beans in bean pot and cover with salt pork pieces. Dissolve salt, mustard, ginger, molasses or sugar, and syrup in some of the reserved water and pour it and rest of reserved water over beans. Add enough boiling water to cover beans with 1 inch. Bake, covered, in 250 degree oven for about 6 hours. Check beans often and add hot water during baking, enough to prevent beans from drying out. Leave top off bean pot for last half hour and increase oven temperature to 300 degrees to brown off and to thicken sauce. About 20 servings.

Submitted by Penny Savage
Mitchell and Savage Maple Syrup, Bowdoin

Gwen Kinney
Kinney's Maple Supplies, Knox

GINGER BAKED BEANS

"Enjoy this delicious recipe developed with tender loving care at the Yellow House Bed, Breakfast, and Catering Company, on Clark's Hill in Oakfield, Maine," writes Gina. She is a neighbor of Kristi and Kevin Brannen, Maine maple and honey producers in Aroostook County, and loves to experiment with their sweet ingredients in her food preparation. When satisfied with the taste test, she enthusiastically serves the dishes to her guests. She has graciously shared some of her favorites.

1 pound Yellow Eye dry beans, sorted and rinsed
1 medium onion, peeled,
    or 1 to 2 teaspoons onion powder and tad of ground clove
About ¼ pound salt pork
    or 2 tablespoons chopped bacon
1 teaspoon prepared or dry mustard
½ teaspoon ground ginger root or ginger
2 tablespoons chopped ginger (in jar)
2 tablespoons catsup
1 tablespoon molasses
1 cup pure Maine maple syrup (Dark or Extra Dark)
½ teaspoon salt and 1/8 ground pepper (to taste)

Soak beans overnight covered with 2 inches of water. In morning change water and bring to boil. Boil for 5 minutes, turn off heat, and cover. Let stand 1 hour. Drain and rinse beans. Pour beans into medium-sized bean pot or 2½ quart baking dish and place onion and salt pork or bacon on top. Mix together mustard, gingers, catsup, molasses, maple syrup, salt, and pepper in a bowl and pour mixture over beans in pot. Add enough water to cover beans one inch. Cover pot. Bake in 250 degree oven for 5 to 6 hours or 350 degrees for 2 to 3 hours, until beans are to a softness that pleases you... (Gina prefers the lower temperature and longer time). Add water as needed. About 10 servings.

Submitted by Gina Clark, Oakfield

QUICK BAKED BEANS

Need an on-the-spot dish for supper or a quick campfire meal while canoe tripping? Try this! It has been one of John's specialties when guiding Boy Scouts, or family and friends down the many wild rivers of Maine. He tops it off with his famous reflector oven biscuits. Just to go for!

Simply delish and nutrish!

    1 can (28 ounces) of baked beans
    ¼ cup pure Maine maple syrup (or to taste)
    ¼ teaspoon dry mustard
    1 teaspoon dried minced onion
    3 or 4 cooked and sliced hot dogs
    1 can (8 ounces) pineapple chunks

Mix all ingredients together in medium-sized casserole dish or saucepan and slowly warm. Serve over campfire biscuits.

Serves 4.

Submitted by John Hodgkins
Jackson Mountain Farm, Temple

CHILI

What to do with the leftover beans? Concocting Gina's and Kristi's chili is an option. Great for lunch or supper after spending time in the grand outdoors on cold days. The maple mellows the spicy bite.

2 pounds natural ground buffalo, beef, pork, or turkey
2 tablespoons olive oil or cooking oil
1 tablespoon freshly minced garlic
1 cup finely chopped sweet onion
½ cup red, yellow, or green chopped pepper (optional)
2 cups fresh or canned tomato sauce
1 large can (3½ cups) chopped tomatoes (optional)
¼ to ½ cup Pure Maine maple syrup (Dark Amber)
1 to 3 tablespoons chili powder (to taste)
1 teaspoon allspice or 1 tablespoon cumin
½ teaspoon fresh ground pepper or cayenne pepper
1 cup of leftover Ginger Baked Beans
    or traditional baked or canned baked beans
4 cups cooked red kidney beans (leftover or canned)

In a stockpot, sauté ground meat in oil and minced garlic. Add onion and fresh pepper, if using. Drain fat and return meat and vegetables to stockpot, if removed. Add tomato sauce, tomatoes (if using), maple syrup, chili powder, allspice or cumin, and black pepper. Bring to boil and simmer for an hour or more. Add kidney and baked beans. Continue to cook only until beans are hot. Take a taste test and season to taste. Serve with a dollop of sour cream or natural corn chips, if desire.

Submitted by Chef Gina Iacoponi Clark
Yellow House B&B, Oakfield

Kristi Brannen
Spring Break Maple & Honey, Smyrna

CREAM OF SQUASH SOUP

A delicious, cold weather soup made with an interesting blend of squash, spices and pure Maine maple syrup. A great second preparation for that leftover squash, also. The toasted croutons add texture and really dress it up for company—or treat your family.

½ cup onion, minced
1 tablespoon butter
2½ cups chicken broth
1 cup cooked winter squash,
    sweetened with a splash of maple syrup
½ teaspoon ground cinnamon
¼ teaspoon garlic powder
¼ teaspoon dry mustard
Salt and pepper to taste
2 tablespoons pure Maine maple syrup
¾ cup cream, whole milk, or skim milk
1 small can sliced mushrooms
Toasted croutons

In a large saucepan, sauté onion in butter until tender. Add 1 cup chicken broth and simmer 10 minutes. Gradually pour into blender and blend thoroughly. Blend in squash. Return mixture to saucepan and add remaining broth, cinnamon, garlic, dry mustard, salt and pepper to taste; bring to boil. Reduce heat; stir until smooth. Add maple syrup, cover and simmer 10 minutes; next add cream or milk. (Do not boil) If milk is used, you may want to add more butter (2 tablespoons). Then add the mushrooms. Serve, topped with toasted croutons. Serves 4.

PORK AND VEGGIE MEDLEY

Pure Maine maple syrup delivers a subtle bouquet and distinct flavor to this pork and vegetable dish. As I was testing my adaptation of the original in my kitchen, my friend Sue stopped by for our daily walk and exclaimed, "My, what's cooking? It smells so good! I bet it has maple in it."

1 pound boned pork loin, cut into ¾ inch cubes
1 to 2 tablespoons olive oil
½ cup onion, chopped
6 ounces canned or 8 ounces fresh mushrooms, sliced
½ cup sweet red pepper, chopped
1¼ cups sliced carrots
2 tablespoons pure Maine maple syrup
½ teaspoon dry thyme
2 cups chicken broth
1 cup apple cider
2 tablespoons cornstarch
2 teaspoons Dijon mustard
 2 teaspoons red wine vinegar
6 to 8 cups cooked brown rice (depending on family)

Sauté pork pieces, half at a time, in olive oil heated in large Dutch oven for 5 minutes. Remove pork from pan. Add onion, mushrooms, and red pepper to pan and sauté 4 minutes. Return pork to pan; add carrots, maple syrup, thyme, broth, and cider. Bring to boil, reduce heat, and simmer until pork is done (about 1 hour). Whisk together cornstarch, vinegar, and mustard in bowl. Add to pork and boil 3 minutes, stirring often. Serve over rice. Serves 8.

For a second preparation, add rice to pork and veggies and serve as a thick stew.

Recipe adapted from *Cooking Light*

VEGETARIAN STIR-FRY

Joe, a young and eager returnee to Temple who is learning the sugaring process at Jackson Mountain's sugarhouse, offers this favorite vegetarian stir-fry recipe that includes ingredients from both sides of the globe. After a day's work in his organic garden, he enjoys whipping up this meal with an Asian flair for himself. "I use pure Maine maple syrup in most everything I cook. It makes it taste good and it's good for me. You can easily double or triple this recipe, if you have a family to feed," he states.

1 tablespoon toasted sesame oil
2 tablespoons pure Maine maple syrup
1½ tablespoons tamari soy sauce
¼ teaspoon turmeric
1/8 teaspoon garam masala
½ thumb-sized piece of ginger, diced
1 large carrot, sliced
½ cup onions, chopped into large chunks
1½ cups broccoli, cut to bite-sized pieces
1 large leaf kale, cut to bite-sized pieces
½ cup firm tofu, cubed

(Stir constantly throughout cooking process.) With wok on high heat, add oil, syrup, soy sauce, turmeric, garam masala, and ginger. Then add carrot, onion, broccoli, kale, and tofu. Turn wok to medium heat and cook vegetables to desired texture. Serve over quinoa and lentils and enjoy. Garnish with pickles, if desire.

Option: Near the end of cooking add 1 tablespoon sesame tahini and 2 teaspoons curry powder. Mix in and cook 5 more minutes.

In saucepan combine 1/8 cup quinoa, 1/8 cup red lentils, pinch of turmeric and 1 inch by 2 inch piece of sea kelp. Add ½ cup water and cook over low boil 25 minutes.

Submitted by Joe Hodgkins
Organic farmer, Temple

 *FARFALLE*

Bill loves to experiment with pure Maine maple syrup now that he has his own kitchen. He shares one of his favorites. He says the maple adds its own character to the dish. Serve with a meat and green salad.

6 ounces bow-tie pasta (farfalle)
1 tablespoon butter
1 medium onion, chopped
1 cup portobello or other fresh mushrooms, sliced
2 cloves garlic, minced
4 cups thinly sliced, fresh spinach
1 teaspoon snipped, fresh basil
1/8 teaspoon crushed black pepper
1 tablespoon pure Maine maple syrup
2 tablespoons shredded Parmesan cheese

Cook pasta according to package directions; drain well. Meanwhile, in a large skillet melt butter over medium heat. Add onion, mushrooms, and garlic. Cook and stir 2 to 3 minutes; until mushrooms nearly tender. Stir in spinach, basil, and pepper and cook 1 more minute or until heated through and spinach is wilted. Stir in maple syrup, then pasta. Toss gently to mix. Sprinkle with cheese. Makes four side dish servings.

Submitted by Bill Hodgkins
Jackson Mountain Farm

(I wonder if Bill, a fifth grader at the time, remembers a neighborhood car pool conversation he had on the way to morning band practice the Thursday before April vacation. His friends excitingly offer, "I'm visiting my grandparents in Pittsburg." "I'm going to Washington, D.C." "I'm going to Disney World!" "Well, I'm going to Temple to wash sap buckets," chimes Bill.)

Judy Harmon

✳ *ITALIAN GARDEN PASTA*

A summer, fall-time favorite—a tasty and nutritious dish to make use of that prolific garden zucchini and broccoli. What a pleasing difference the maple makes.

½ box ziti
2 cups cooked chicken, chunked
½ cup chopped green pepper
1 cup sliced mushrooms, canned or fresh
1 cup sliced or cubed zucchini
1 cup cut-up broccoli
1 cup sliced celery
1 tablespoon olive oil
1 tablespoon soy sauce
2 tablespoons pure Maine maple syrup
28 ounce jar garlic/onion pasta sauce,
      or 3 ½ cups of homemade sauce
Grated mozzarella cheese

Cook ziti according to package directions. Meanwhile, stir-fry chicken, green pepper, mushrooms, zucchini, broccoli, celery, soy sauce, and maple syrup in oil. When vegetables are tender-crunchy, add the pasta sauce and heat.

To serve, spread ziti on platter and cover with pasta sauce. Sprinkle with grated mozzarella cheese and melt under broiler a very few minutes. (Watch carefully.) Or place in warm oven a few minutes. Serves 4 to 6.

115

VIII

VEGETABLES

Vegetables add flavor, color, and crunch to our meals as well as healthy nutrients. Dress them with a splash of mellow sweetness—pure Maine maple syrup—to enhance their unique flavors. It will surprise the family—dinner guests, too.

MAPLE GLAZED SQUASH

Squash—that so nutritious winter vegetable! Add pure Maine maple syrup to create deliciousness!

For an elegant touch to our Christmas dinner, Victoria adds a sprinkling of raisins with the maple syrup and butter to each center. Extraordinaire!

Here are two different methods for cooking the squash.

1 medium buttercup or acorn squash (or 2 small ones)
½ cup pure Maine maple syrup
¼ cup butter

Wash squash and cut in half. Scoop out seeds. Place cut sides down in glass baking dish. Add ½ cup of water and cover with plastic wrap. Microwave 8 to 10 minutes until squash is tender. Remove plastic wrap. Melt butter and add maple syrup to the butter. Brush cut sides and top of squash with syrup mixture. Place cut side up onto baking dish and microwave 2 to 3 minutes more to glaze the squash. Season to taste with salt and pepper.

Submitted by Dianne Haulk
Haulk's Maple, Madison

Or you can place the uncooked squash cut side up, spoon the maple syrup mixture into the centers and season to taste with salt and pepper. Add ½ inch water to bottom of dish, cover with foil, and bake in 350 degree oven until tender (between 30 and 45 minutes, depending on size of squash.)

Submitted by SMMSA

For mashed squash add a splash of maple along with other seasonings and butter.

CABBAGE AND APPLES

The crunch of the cabbage and apple is a delight and so tasty served with ham or herb seasoned chicken, pork, or beef. "For a wonderful one-dish supper, add left-over chicken or ham to the cabbage and apples," Chef Harry suggests. Just try it! It's delish!

.

1 tablespoon olive oil
1 medium onion, minced
2 tart green apples (Cortlands work as well)
1 (1 pound) red cabbage, shredded (green works, too)
1/3 cup brandy, wine, or apple juice
2/3 cup pure Maine maple syrup
Salt and pepper to taste

In large saucepan or 6-quart Dutch oven over medium-high heat, add oil and sauté onion until golden. Core and cut up apples. Add to onion and sauté 1 to 2 minutes. Place cabbage in pan and drizzle brandy, wine or apple juice over cabbage. Sauté gently until cabbage begins to wilt. Stir in maple syrup and seasoning. Serve hot. Makes 8 servings.

Shared by Chef Harry Schwartz
Television personality, author, food columnist

MAPLE BAKED ONIONS

A favorite from the Bacon Farm.

Layer 6 large, sweet onions, sliced ½ inch thick, in greased 13 x 9 inch baking dish. Combine 1/3 cup maple syrup with ¼ cup melted butter. Pour over onions. Bake in 425 degree oven 40 to 45 minutes, until tender.

Submitted by Shelley Bacon
Bacon Farm Maple Products, Sidney

CARROTS

A great company dish!

6 medium-sized carrots, sliced
3 tablespoons butter, melted
3 tablespoons pure Maine maple syrup
½ teaspoon ginger
Salt to taste

Cook carrots until crunchy tender. Mix butter, ginger, and maple syrup, add to carrots; salt to taste. Then simmer until glazed. Serves 4.

Submitted by SMMSA

BAKED APPLES AND CARROTS

This dish complements a pork roast, fish, chicken....

4 large carrots, peeled and sliced
2 medium tart apples, peeled and sliced thinly
2 tablespoons pure Maine maple syrup
2 tablespoons brown sugar
2 tablespoons butter
Dash salt

Put carrots and apples into a 1½ quart buttered baking dish. Mix together maple syrup and brown sugar and pour over carrots and apples. Add salt. Dot with butter. Bake uncovered until apples are fork tender, about 1 hour, in 375 degree oven. Stir a couple of times during cooking. Serves 4 to 6.

Adaptation from *Maple Cooking* by Beatrice Vaughan

SWEET POTATO SPEARS

What are sweet potatoes without pure Maine maple? A real treat served with chicken, fish or pork. Packed with nutrients!

"Where did you get these? No, did you really make them?" asks my husband the first time I served them. "By gosh! They're good."

1 large (about 12 ounces) sweet potato, peeled
2 teaspoons olive oil
Salt to taste
2 tablespoons pure Maine maple syrup
1 teaspoon cider vinegar
¼ teaspoon dried thyme

Preheat oven to 425 degrees. Cut potato in half, lengthwise; slice each half into 4 spears, ¾ to 1 inch wide. Roll spears in 1 teaspoon oil and salt, and place spears on lightly oiled baking pan. Roast until tender (about 25 minutes), turning once.

Meanwhile, mix together maple syrup, vinegar, and 1 teaspoon oil. Brush over spears and return to oven to caramelize, about 10 minutes. Remove from oven and sprinkle with thyme. Serves 2.

If there are any spears leftover, they make a great addition to a veggie stew. Just cube and pop them into a ready-made soup.

CANDIED SWEET POTATOES

This recipe is my adaptation from Fanny Farmer Cookbook. One evening I served them to our son-in-law, Bob Stephens. "You know, I generally don't like sweet potatoes," he commented, "but, boy, are these good." I had no leftovers that meal. Share the oven with baked fish, chicken, pork.

1 large (about 12 ounces) sweet potato
1 tablespoon butter
2 tablespoons pure Maine maple syrup
Salt to taste

Cut potato into chunks. Boil until tender but firm. Cool, peel, and cut into ½ inch cubes.
While oven is preheating to 300 degrees, melt butter with maple syrup in glass pie plate or small baking dish placed in oven. Remove baking dish from oven and coat potato cubes with butter and syrup. Cover with foil, and bake slowly until cubes are heated through. Serves 2.

Variation: Increase the maple syrup by 1 tablespoon, add a peeled and sliced apple with a few pecans to the baking dish and sprinkle all with a dash of nutmeg just before you pop the dish into the oven.

121

SWEET POTATO CASSERROLE

After living in Maine for several years, Mary has discovered that Maine maple greatly enhances her southern cooking as well as her southern hospitality.

This casserole, as is, is delicious; or you can jazz it up by topping it with crumbled cooked bacon and chopped fresh rosemary, sautéed onion and garlic, or chopped smoked almonds before baking. The dish can conveniently share the oven with chicken, pork tenderloin, or fish while baking.

1/3 cup yellow cornmeal
1½ cups skim milk
2 tablespoons butter
2 cups cooked and mashed sweet potato (about 1¼ pounds)
1/3 cup pure Maine maple syrup
½ teaspoon salt
½ teaspoon cinnamon
¼ teaspoon allspice
¼ teaspoon black pepper
2 eggs, lightly beaten
Cooking spray

Place cornmeal in a medium saucepan. Gradually add milk, stirring with wire whisk until blended. Bring to boil; reduce heat to medium. Stirring constantly with wire whisk, cook, uncovered for 2 minutes. Remove from heat, stir in butter. Set aside.

Combine mashed sweet potato, maple syrup, salt, cinnamon, allspice, pepper, and eggs in a large bowl. Blend well. Gradually add cornmeal mixture, stirring constantly. Pour sweet potato mixture into a 1½ quart casserole coated with cooking spray. Bake at 350 degrees for 40 minutes. Let stand 10 minutes before serving. Serves 8.

Submitted by Mary Stuart, Yarmouth
Friend of Jackson Mountain Farm

BRUSSELS SPROUTS AND SWEET POTATO

This recipe is an interesting combo of nutrition and flavors blended with maple. Serve with baked chicken or salmon and a green salad.

2 strips bacon, cut into ½ inch pieces
½ onion, finely chopped
¾ -1 pound brussels sprouts, thinly sliced
Salt and pepper to taste
½ cup toasted pecans, coarsely chopped (optional)
1 large sweet potato (about 1 pound), peeled and thinly sliced
3 tablespoons pure Maine maple syrup, Dark Amber preferred
1 tablespoon butter, melted

Preheat oven to 400 degrees. In skillet, cook bacon over medium heat until crisp. Remove bacon and drain on paper towel. Spoon out extra fat, if any.

Reduce heat to low, add onion, and cook until translucent, about 5 minutes. Add brussels sprouts and cook, stirring frequently until tender (about 5 minutes). Remove to bowl and add bacon, salt, pepper, and pecans to brussels sprouts.

Add sweet potato slices to skillet and cook until light brown (about 3 minutes a side).

Whisk together maple syrup and butter. Toss all ingredients together in a lightly greased baking dish and bake 20 minutes. Serves 3 or 4.

An adaption of a recipe published in The Maple News.
Submitted by Tom Bivins, Executive Chef
The Old Tavern, Grafton, Vermont

EGGPLANT AND SUMMER SQUASH DISH

A palate-pleasing way to use those prolific, late summer, early fall vegetables. Guests will savor them! Maple makes the difference.

Serve with a grilled meat, garden salad, and rolls or whole-grain bread. Yes!

1 medium zucchini, summer squash,
            or a small one of each, cut into 1/2 inch cubes
1 medium eggplant, peeled and cut into 1/2 inch cubes
4 tomatoes, peeled and diced
1 tablespoon pure Maine maple syrup
1 onion, chopped
1 tablespoon olive oil
Garlic, basil, salt, pepper to taste
¼ cup parmesan cheese, grated

In saucepan boil squash and eggplant in salted water for 3 minutes and drain. Add tomatoes and maple syrup.

In skillet, sauté onion in oil until tender. Add garlic, basil, salt, and pepper plus the vegetable and syrup mixture to the skillet. Simmer gently, uncovered, until vegetables are crisp tender.

Pour mixture into casserole dish and sprinkle with parmesan cheese. Carefully brown under broiler to melt cheese. Makes 4 servings.

124

STIR-FRY SUMMER VEGGIES

Another appetizing dish that takes advantage of the summer harvest. Soy and Maine maple combine to give it a softened bite for interest. Serve over rice with maple-glazed chicken or pork hot off the grill.

1 tablespoon olive oil
1 carrot, finely chopped
¼ cup onion, finely chopped
1 small zucchini, finely chopped
1 small summer squash, finely chopped
¼ cup red pepper, finely chopped
2 teaspoons soy sauce
2 teaspoons pure Maine maple syrup
Salt and pepper to taste

Pour oil in skillet and stir-fry carrot and onion 3 minutes. Add zucchini, summer squash and red pepper. Stir-fry 3 more minutes. Add soy sauce and maple syrup. Stir to coat. Salt and pepper to taste.
Serves 2.

HARVARD BEETS

The evening before heading north for sugaring—we'll be gone for two months—I clean out the fridge for our last meal at home. I find cooked beets from two suppers ago. I ponder, "These won't enhance our evening meal!" My conservative Yankeeism—passed on from my folks who were survivors of the Great Depression— clutters my mind. "I can't run these through the garbage disposal," I think. Then my memory bank opens. "Mom's Harvard beets!" I yank down her antique wooden box and skim her red stained recipe. My eyes stop at the word sugar.
"Ah, ha!"

Here's Mom's "new" recipe. Try it. You won't use white sugar to make Harvard beets again.

> 6 tablespoons pure Maine maple syrup
> 1 tablespoon cornstarch
> Salt to taste (about ½ teaspoon)
> 1/3 cup vinegar
> ¼ cup boiling water
> 1 to 2 teaspoons butter
> 2 cups sliced, cooked beets

Mix maple syrup, cornstarch, and salt together. Add vinegar and boiling water and cook until clear. Add butter and beets; keep warm for 30 minutes. Serves 2 to 4.

An adaption of Wilma Gamage's
Harvard Beets recipe

IX

SALADS

A few hundred years ago the French and Spanish introduced salads to America. Today they are an important dish in our daily menus. They help balance a meal with nutrition, texture, color, taste, and beauty. Salads are an appetizer, an accompaniment, or a main dish for lunch or supper.

Betty Crocker Picture Cookbook
First Edition

Pure Maine maple syrup as a salad ingredient? By all means! The chemistry of maple syrup paired with citrus juices and vinegars, plus spices in various dressings adds a vim and vigor to salads. However, at the same time it mellows the sharpness and blends the flavors. A dribble of maple syrup added to the dressing will make a salad shine.

WALDORF STYLE SALAD

This Waldorf version is dressed with a tangy orange, maple, and yogurt dressing. Serve to complement chicken, beef stew, or baked beans at dinner, or as a summer-time lunch on a bed of lettuce with cottage cheese and a slice of homemade bread. Delish!

1 Granny Smith apple, diced into ½ inch cubes
1 cup chunked pineapple, fresh or canned
½ cup seedless red grapes, halved
1 rib celery, cut into ¼ inch dices
¼ cup coarsely chopped or slivered almonds

Mix all ingredients together in bowl and add dressing.
Serves 3 or 4.

Dressing:

½ cup non-fat plain yogurt
½ cup low fat mayonnaise
2 tablespoons orange syrup (recipe below)
Zest of 1 orange

Mix all ingredients and refrigerate until needed.

Orange syrup:

1 cup fresh orange juice
1 tablespoon pure Maine maple syrup

Combine juice and maple syrup in small saucepan and bring to boil. Lower heat and cook, uncovered, stirring frequently for 10 to 15 minutes, until thickens. Should have about ¾ cup of syrup when done. Cool and store in refrigerator.

Can be used as a dessert topping, also.

FRESH CITRUS SALAD

Add spark, fiber, and vitamin C to your meal with this salad. It pairs well with the Chicken Stir-Fry in the" Meat, Fish, Poultry" section. Also, chunked apple may be substituted for the grapefruit.

A tasty make-ahead salad.

1 cup grapefruit sections or chunked apple pieces
1 cup orange sections
1 tablespoon orange zest
¼ cup slivered almonds

Combine grapefruit or apple, orange, and zest in mixing bowl. Add dressing. Cover and chill for 1 hour. When ready to serve, sprinkle in the almonds. Serves 4.

Dressing:

2 tablespoons pure Maine maple syrup (or 1 tablespoon of maple
                    syrup and 1 tablespoon of orange juice)
2 tablespoons sesame seeds (optional)
1/8 teaspoon salt
8 ounces plain low-fat yogurt or mayonnaise

Blend together.

Dressing for Waldorf Style Salad on previous page is also good on this salad.

BETHEL'S CALICO SLAW

This salad, packed with color and crunch, is one of my favorite summer salads. It complements most any meal fresh off the grill, plus it is a prepare-ahead-of-time salad. Perfect for a backyard gathering of family and friends.

5 cups shredded green cabbage
2 cups red cabbage
2 cups tiny broccoli flowerets
1 medium carrot, grated
2 tablespoons minced onion,
            or 1 teaspoon dried minced onion (to taste)
2 tablespoons chopped sweet red pepper

Toss vegetables together in large bowl. Dress with recipe below and chill in refrigerator. It serves 6 to 8 easily; but, of course, it can be halved for a smaller group.

Dressing:

2/3 cup canola oil (or less)
1/3 cup cider vinegar
2 teaspoons Dijon mustard (to taste)
2 teaspoons pure Maine maple syrup
2 dashes salt (or to taste)

Whisk together and pour over salad. (Can be made a day ahead and stored in refrigerator.)

Submitted by Bethel H. Stephens
Jackson Mountain Farm

CABBAGE AND APPLE SALAD

When fall rolls around, this is a favorite. It is a make-ahead salad, also. So convenient for those busy days.

Bob Stephens, Bethel's taster, raves about the salad. "This is the best cabbage salad I've ever eaten, Bethel. What's in it that makes it so good? You just have to get your mom's recipe!"
In reality it's Bethel's recipe. I just added maple syrup to the dressing.

4 cups shredded cabbage
1 cup grated carrot
2 stalks celery, chopped
½ cup chopped tart red apple, or finely chopped cucumber
½ teaspoon dried minced onion
Dash salt

Mix vegetables and salt in large bowl. Toss with dressing recipe below, cover tightly, and refrigerate at least a couple hours for the dressing to penetrate. Serves 4 to 6.

Dressing:

1/3 cup Miracle Whip or mayonnaise
2 tablespoons cider vinegar
1 teaspoon Dijon mustard
2 teaspoons pure Maine maple syrup
Dash salt

Whisk together and pour over above salad.

An adaptation of Bethel's Calico Slaw.

MUSHROOM SALAD WITH MAPLE DRESSING

This recipe was submitted by Penny Savage of Mitchell and Savage Maple Syrup and Val Vaughan, a Cornell University graduate with a major in foods and journalism and a former backyard maple producer. Val and Penny love to mess in the kitchen. And, believe me, their creations always require a second trip to the buffet table. This salad is no exception!

2 tablespoons lime juice
2 tablespoons pure Maine maple syrup
¼ teaspoon low-sodium soy sauce
¼ teaspoon sesame oil
1/8 teaspoon black pepper
1½ teaspoons salad oil
Cooking spray
8 ounces button mushrooms, sliced
6 cups torn salad greens, such as "spring mix"
1/3 cup chopped green onion (optional)
1 tablespoon finely chopped, fresh parsley or cilantro
(optional)

Whisk together lime juice, maple syrup, soy sauce, sesame oil, and pepper. Heat salad oil in large skillet over medium heat. Add mushrooms and sauté for 6 minutes or until tender. Remove from heat and add maple mixture, toss to coat. Combine greens, onions, and herbs in bowl and add mushroom mixture. Toss and serve immediately. Serves 4.

Submitted by Penny Savage
Mitchell and Savage Maple Syrup, Bowdoin

Valerie Vaughan
A former backyard maple producer, Yarmouth

SPINACH AND PEAR SALAD

A great first course or with-the-meal salad. Apples work well, also.

1 pear, cut into 15-16 slices
8 cups torn fresh spinach (green lettuce works)
¼ thinly sliced red onion (optional)
Craisins and walnuts (optional)
Parmesan cheese

Put pear slices in a large bowl. Pour 1 tablespoon of dressing over them and coat. Add spinach and onions and rest of dressing and toss. Serve in individual bowls and sprinkle with craisins, walnuts and parmesan cheese, if desire. Serves 4 to 6.

Dressing:

2 tablespoons water
1½ tablespoons red wine vinegar
1 tablespoon olive oil
1 tablespoon pure Maine maple syrup
2 teaspoons Dijon mustard
¼ teaspoon celery seeds

Whisk all ingredients together.

MAPLIZED NUTS

As I prepared the Spinach and Pear Salad for New Year's Eve guests, I wondered, "Why not maplized nuts?" So . . . I put a ½ cup mixed nuts and 2 tablespoons of pure Maine maple syrup into a small non-stick skillet and gave them a shake of salt. I cooked them over medium-high heat for 3 to 4 minutes, stirring frequently, and then tasted. Aah, crunchy and flavorful—maplized, too. Also use on cereals, frosted cakes, ice cream . . . or just nibble. (Store in air-tight jar in refrigerator.)

SPINACH AND APPLE SALAD

Packed with nutrition, fiber, texture, color and a variety of favorite flavors, this salad can be the focus of a delightful summertime lunch or light supper. Complete the meal with a maple roll or a slice of whole-grain bread.

6 cups spinach or part lettuce,
        washed, torn, and de-stemmed
1 large red apple, cored and sliced into 16 thin slices
½ cup cubed ham or chicken pieces or crisp bacon pieces
1 large hard-boiled egg, peeled and chopped
1 cup sharp cheddar cheese, grated or cubed

Place spinach (or lettuce, if using), apple, meat, and egg into salad bowl. Whisk together salad dressing from recipe below. When ready to serve, drizzle about half of the warmed dressing over ingredients in bowl and toss. Then add cheese and rest of dressing and toss again. Serve immediately. Serves 4 to 6.

Dressing:

1/3 cup pure Maine maple syrup
1/3 cup cider vinegar (more or less to taste)
Dash salt
Shake of black pepper

When ready to serve salad, whisk all ingredients together in glass measuring cup and zap in micro or pour into a small pan to warm over low heat. (Dressing keeps for a couple of weeks stored in the refrigerator.)

BROCCOLI SALAD

Need a veggie to balance out your meal on a hot summer evening? Prepare this crunchy, but tasty and healthy salad in the cool of the morning, and you can enjoy the social hour on the back patio with family and friends while the meat is grilling.

"This is a variation of a well-known recipe. Substituting pure Maine maple syrup for the sugar makes it much better!" exclaims Edwina Hardy, Mountain Maple from Rumford.

1 bunch broccoli, chopped to bite-sized pieces
½ head cauliflower, cut-up (optional)
½ cup finely chopped sweet onion
½ cup raisins
¼ cup bacon, fried and crumbled,
          or bacon bits
(Also optional—add ½ cup chopped, sweet red pepper
              ¼ cup sunflower seeds)

Toss all ingredients together in bowl. Coat with dressing below and refrigerate for at least an hour, more is better, before serving.
Serves 4 to 6.

Dressing:

1 to 1½ cups mayonnaise
2-4 tablespoons pure Maine maple syrup (to taste)
3 tablespoons balsamic or red wine vinegar

Whisk together all ingredients, pour over salad and chill.

Submitted by Edwina Hardy
Mountain Maple, Rumford

BEAN AND CORN SALAD

*Having guests for an informal meal or need a salad for a potluck?
Here is another prepare-ahead recipe that is quick to make, easy to
transport, and a pleasing complement to the hot and spicy grilled
meats. The maple cuts the sharp edge of the lime juice and vinegar.
And you won't have to serve leftovers later. It does, however, keep
well in the refrigerator for a couple of days. "And you can make it
into a meal-in-one dish by topping with strips of grilled chicken,"
adds Val.*

1 can (16 ounces) kidney beans, rinsed and drained
1 can (16 ounces) black beans, rinsed and drained
1 can (10 ounces) whole-kernel corn, drained
1 green bell pepper, finely chopped
1 red bell pepper, finely chopped
4 ½ tablespoons lime juice
3 tablespoons olive oil
3 tablespoons cider vinegar
2 tablespoons pure Maine maple syrup
1 teaspoon dried, minced onion or 3 chives chopped
Black pepper to taste
2 tablespoons finely chopped parsley or cilantro (optional)

In a large bowl combine beans, corn, and green and red
peppers. Whisk together lime juice, oil, vinegar, maple syrup,
and onion or chives. Pour over vegetables and mix well. Cover
and refrigerate for at least 2 hours to let flavors blend. I like
to stir it a couple of times while chilling. Just before serving,
season with black pepper. If you like, garnish with parsley or
cilantro.

Submitted by Val Vaughan, Yarmouth
Former backyard maple producer

An adaptation from *Grilling/Food Writers' Favorites*

SALMON SALAD

A second preparation for that leftover salmon. Salmon salad works well for lunch served on a bed of lettuce with crackers or toast and fruit, or for supper with a hot vegetable and a favorite bread or roll.

1 pound grilled salmon, chilled over night
1 cup vegetables and fruit (or more to your liking)
    celery, green pepper, onion, broccoli flowerets, apple

In medium-sized bowl flake salmon into bite-sized chunks. Cut vegetables and apple into bite-sized pieces and mix with salmon. Add dressing (recipe below) and mix well. Chill an hour or more. Serve on a bed of lettuce. Makes 2 to 3 servings.

Dressing:

2 tablespoons fresh dill or 1 teaspoon of dried
2 tablespoons olive oil
2 tablespoons mayonnaise
2 tablespoons red wine vinegar or balsamic vinegar
2 tablespoons pure Maine maple syrup

Whisk all ingredients together and mix into salmon mixture.

This dressing is also delicious tossed with green salad.

MAPLE-DIJON-BACON DRESSING

"Great on salads with spinach and bitter greens such as radicchio, escarole or endive. Tasty additions to the greens are bacon, carrots, tomatoes, and onion," suggests Chef Jody.

½ cup pure Maine maple syrup, Dark or Extra Dark
1 tablespoon Dijon mustard
¼ cup white wine vinegar
Bacon fat (whatever is available)
Neutral oil (canola or other vegetable oil)
2 tablespoons olive oil
      (the sum of the oils and fat should equal ¾ cup)
Salt and black pepper to taste

All ingredients should be at room temperature, except the bacon fat, which should be a bit warmer.

Reduce the amount of syrup to 1/3 cup by slightly simmering it on low heat. (This is to thicken it.) Cool a bit. Mix it with mustard, vinegar, dashes of salt and pepper until it is well blended. Add bacon fat in a slow stream, whisking constantly. Add other oils (olive oil last). Whisk lightly. Check seasoning.

Submitted by Jody Haynes
Chef/food connoisseur

138

MAPLE VINEGRETTE

"This recipe is my all-time favorite!" exclaims Gina. "Nothing tops a maple/balsamic combo when it comes to dressings. I try to keep a jar of it pre-made in the refrigerator, but I keep running out." Savory on tossed salads.

    4 tablespoons balsamic or red wine vinegar
    1 teaspoon dry mustard
    1 teaspoon dried basil
    4 tablespoons pure Maine maple syrup
    1 tablespoon lemon juice
    1 clove garlic, minced or 1/8 teaspoon garlic powder
    1 cup olive oil (or less)
    1 teaspoon salt (or to taste)
    ½ teaspoon black pepper (to taste)

Whisk vinegar, mustard, basil, and maple syrup together in a small bowl. Add lemon juice, garlic, and oil and whisk until well blended. Season with salt and pepper to taste. Makes 1¼ cups.

Submitted by Chef Gina Iacoponi Clark
Yellow House B&B, Oakfield

QUICK DRESSING FOR GREENS

Another tasty dressing for salad greens that keeps well in the refrigerator. So convenient to have for that last minute salad.

    ¾ cup canola or vegetable oil (or less)
    ¼ cup cider vinegar
    2 tablespoons pure Maine maple syrup
    1 teaspoon mustard
    ½ teaspoon paprika
    Whisk together. Season to taste. Makes 1 cup.

Submitted by SMMSA

TOMATO KETCHUP DRESSING

This is a sweet and sour tomato dressing that is delicious on a green garden salad or a spinach, boiled egg, and mushroom salad.

½ cup tomato ketchup
½ cup or less vegetable oil
½ cup pure Maine maple syrup
1 teaspoon dry mustard
2 tablespoons lemon juice
2 tablespoons relish (optional)
1 rib celery, chopped fine
1 green onion, chopped or onion powder to taste
1 clove garlic, chopped or garlic powder to taste
6 tablespoons cider vinegar
Salt to taste

Combine all ingredients in a blender and mix thoroughly, or put them in a 2 to 3 cup jar and shake. Keeps in refrigerator for 2 weeks or more.

Adapted from recipe submitted by

Danielle Rodrigue
Quebec

Martine Pruveau
Maple Mountain Products, Quebec

Sylvie Pare
Quebec

Chantal Gilbert
Quebec

X

DESSERTS

Ah, desserts! Pure Maine maple syrup or pure Maine maple sugar "turn the simplest desserts into masterpieces. Its delicate flavor enhances—not to be rivaled in the field."

Beatrice Vaughan
Real, Old-time Yankee Maple Cooking

We've nourished our bodies with nutritious and scrumptious foods—fruits, vegetables, whole grains, meats, fish, poultry— prepared from recipes included in the previous sections of this book. Now it's time to feed our spirit!

Naturally fatty foods such as cream, butter, and nuts accent pure Maine maple syrup's genuine flavor and sweetness. They create magic. Let's try some.

We have collected a wide variety of desserts from the simple and easy for family meals to the elegant and delectable for special occasions. Of course, it's the maple that makes them all succulently divine! We hope they'll bring to each meal or occasion a tasty and delightful "finis".

Enjoy!

CAKES

I baked a cake and my, it was good!
It rose and it browned, as all cakes should.
I made some tea, fragrant and strong.
But that day no one came along!

I made a cake and it was punk!
It rose and then went kerplunk.
I made some tea, both weak and thin
And on that day all our friends dropped in!

Anonymous

MAPLE SYRUP LOAF CAKE

*This makes a small, light and gentle cake. Frost with Maple
Butter Frosting (recipe at end of this section) or serve with Berry
or Warm Peach Sauce found in the "Toppings, Glazes, Sauces,
Spreads" section and top with a dollop of whipped cream.*

1 egg
½ cup pure Maine maple syrup
½ cup milk or cream
1 teaspoon vanilla extract
2 tablespoons canola or vegetable oil
1 cup flour
1½ teaspoons baking powder
¾ teaspoon salt

Preheat oven to 350 degrees. Beat egg in mixing bowl. Stir in
maple syrup, milk, vanilla, and oil. Sift together flour, baking
powder, and salt; add to liquids. Beat until mixed. Pour into a
greased loaf pan or 8-inch square pan and bake 30-40 minutes.

Submitted by SMMSA

THE ULTIMATE BIRTHDAY CAKE

John notes, "For the first few years after Beth and I were married, her mother continued the tradition of making Beth's birthday cake. But after we moved farther away, and she was unable to deliver the cake timely, I became the heir of the annual tradition. To quell Mother Gamage's anxiety concerning my cake-baking skills, I switched from her traditional white cake recipe to a Maine maple syrup cake, a recipe with which she had had no experience—she loved it."

Taken from the 1950 edition of Betty Crocker's Picture Cookbook this prize-winning recipe dates back three generations prior to 1950.

5 tablespoons butter
5 tablespoons shortening
7/8 cup sugar
2 large eggs
2 ¾ cups sifted flour
2 ½ teaspoons baking powder
1 teaspoon salt
1 cup pure Maine maple syrup
½ cup plus 2 tablespoons milk

Pre-heat oven 350 degrees. Grease and flour two 8-inch or 9-inch round cake pans. Cream together butter, shortening, and sugar. Beat in eggs. Sift together flour, baking powder, and salt; and add to creamed mixture alternately with maple syrup and milk. Mix until uniform. Pour into pans and bake until done (20 to 25 minutes). Cool on racks. Frost with Maple Butter Frosting; recipe found at the end of this section.

Submitted by John Hodgkins
Jackson Mountain Farm, Temple

CARROT CAKE

Always a favorite! The tongue will smile at its gentle sweetness!

4 eggs
1 cup pure Maine maple syrup
1 cup oil
½ cup sour cream
1 tablespoon lemon juice
2 teaspoons vanilla extract
2 cups unbleached flour
2 teaspoons baking soda
½ teaspoon baking powder
¼ teaspoon allspice
2 teaspoons cinnamon
½ teaspoon salt
Zest from 1 orange (optional)
1 cup raisins (optional)
1 cup walnuts, chopped (optional)
2 cups grated carrots

Preheat oven to 350 degrees. Lightly grease a tube pan, or a
9 x 13 inch baking pan. In a medium-sized mixing bowl, beat
eggs 1 minute, until frothy. Continue to beat while adding
maple syrup, oil, sour cream, lemon juice and vanilla gradually.
Combine flour, baking soda, baking powder, allspice, cinnamon,
salt, zest, raisins, and walnuts in a large mixing bowl. Add
liquids to dry ingredients and stir until smooth. Fold in carrots.
Bake for about 1 hour, if using tube pan, or until done. Less, if
using 9 x 13 inch pan. Let cool in pan until easy to handle, turn
onto rack and continue to cool. Frost with Maple Cream Cheese
Frosting or Maple Butter Frosting. (Recipes found at end of this
section.)

BUTTERCUP SQUASH CAKE

A must-try cake! It will become a favorite. It's light and fluffy; delicate to the bite. And the mellow blend of maple syrup and spices tempt the taste buds. A dollop of Maple Whipped Cream is the finishing touch.

1 cup pure Maine maple syrup
½ cup butter, softened
2 eggs
2 cups flour
¼ teaspoon baking soda
2 teaspoons baking powder
½ teaspoon nutmeg
¼ teaspoon cloves
½ teaspoon cinnamon
½ teaspoon salt
¼ cup sour cream
¾ to 1 cup cooked and pureed or mashed squash

Preheat oven to 350 degrees. Cream together maple syrup and butter. Beat in eggs. Combine flour, baking soda, baking powder, nutmeg, cloves, cinnamon, and salt. Beat dry ingredients into creamed mixture alternately with sour cream and squash. Pour into greased and floured 9-inch square pan and bake for about 30 minutes, until done. Serve warm with whipped cream or cooled and frosted with Maple Butter Frosting. (Recipe found at the end of this section.)

(A great way to use that last serving of squash that no one would eat at dinner.)

FROSTINGS, ICINGS, AND WHIPPED CREAM

MAPLE BUTTER FROSTING

Devine on maple, carrot, and vanilla cakes or sugar cookies.

1/3 cup butter, softened
3 cups confectioners' sugar
½ cup pure Maine maple syrup,
    Medium or Dark Amber

Cream butter and confectioners' sugar. Add maple syrup; beat until creamy. Frosts a layer cake or 9 x 12 inch cake.

MAPLE CREAM CHEESE FROSTING

Delightful on carrot cake, or a traditional pumpkin cake, also. Sprinkle frosted cake with chopped nuts, if desire. Frosts a large one.

8 ounces cream cheese, softened (not fat-free)
4 tablespoons butter, softened
6 tablespoons pure Maine maple syrup
1 teaspoon vanilla extract
4 cups confectioners' sugar
½ cup finely chopped walnuts (optional)

In a medium-sized mixing bowl combine cream cheese, butter, maple syrup, and vanilla and beat on low speed until smooth. Gradually add confectioners' sugar and beat to spreading consistency. Store in refrigerator.

BOILED ICING

1 egg white, unbeaten
2/3 cup brown sugar, slightly compressed
½ cup pure Maine maple syrup
Dash of salt
4 drops vanilla extract
½ teaspoon baking powder

Mix in top of double boiler or saucepan over boiling water the egg, sugar, maple syrup, and salt. Beat constantly with an electric mixer until the icing sticks together, about 7 minutes. Take off heat and beat in vanilla and baking powder. Spread onto cooled cake.

Submitted by Chantal Gilbert
Quebec

QUICK MAPLE ICING

1 tablespoon butter, softened
½ teaspoon vanilla extract
2 cups confectioners' sugar
Pure Maine maple syrup

Blend butter, vanilla, and sugar. Add syrup to preferred consistency for spreading on cookies or drizzling over sweet breads or cakes.

MAPLE WHIPPED CREAM

1 cup heavy cream (or whipping cream)
3 tablespoons pure Maine maple syrup
Pinch of salt

Mix and beat all together until stiff. A perfect dessert topping.

COOKIES

"Fill the cookie jar with sweet and chewy memories."

Betty Crocker Picture Cookbook

WHOOPIE PIE COOKIES

"I like to use these to make whoopie pie-like cookies,"
shares Terri. The kids will gobble them up.

½ cup melted butter
1 cup pure Maine maple syrup
1 egg, beaten
2 cups flour
2 teaspoons baking powder
Dash salt (optional)

Preheat oven to 350 degrees. Stir butter and maple syrup
together. Add egg. Sift flour, baking powder, and salt together.
Stir into wet ingredients and let set for 5 minutes. Drop by
spoonfuls onto greased cookie sheets and bake for about 8
minutes. Cool on rack. Use filling recipe to create whoopie
pie-like cookies or simply frost individual cookies.

Filling or Frosting:

2 cups confectioners' sugar
1 tablespoon milk
Pure Maine maple syrup

Put sugar into mixing bowl and add milk and enough maple
syrup to preferred consistency.

Submitted by Terri Sanborne
SMMSA

SUGAR COOKIES

A roll-out cookie for fun. Frost with maple cream or decorate for a holiday. Gather the kids or grandkids, get out their favorite cookie cutters, and have a good old-fashioned bonding time!

1 cup white sugar and ½ cup maple sugar or
      1½ cups white sugar
1 cup butter-flavor Crisco
2 eggs, beaten
¼ cup pure Maine maple syrup, (Medium Amber)
2 to 3 teaspoons vanilla extract
3 cups flour
¾ teaspoon baking powder
½ teaspoon baking soda
½ teaspoon salt
Maple Cream (Optional. Recipe found in "Toppings, Glazes,
      Sauces, Spreads" section.)

Cream together sugar (s) and Crisco. Add eggs, syrup, and vanilla; and beat until well blended and fluffy. Combine flour, baking powder, baking soda, and salt; and gradually add to creamed mixture. If dough is too sticky to handle, wrap in plastic wrap and refrigerate for an hour or so. Roll out to about ¼ inch thickness and cut with cookie cutters. Place 2 inches apart on greased cookie sheet. Bake 5 to 9 minutes in 375 degree oven. Cool 2 minutes on cookie sheet and remove cookies to cookie rack to continue cooling. When completely cool, top with a small dollop of Maple Cream. (Do not cover cookies until cream is set.) Or decorate, if desire. Makes between 3 and 4 dozen.

Submitted by Sue Smith
Smith Brothers Maple, Skowhegan

Diane Haulk
Haulk's Maple, Madison

LACE COOKIES

Deliciously delicate!

1 cup sifted flour
1 cup chopped walnuts or shredded coconut
½ cup pure Maine maple syrup
½ cup brown sugar, firmly packed
½ cup butter
1 teaspoon vanilla extract

Preheat oven to 350 degrees. Mix flour and walnuts or coconut and set aside. Combine maple syrup, brown sugar, and butter in heavy saucepan. Over medium heat bring syrup mixture to boil, stirring constantly. Remove from heat and gradually blend flour and nut mixture into syrup mixture. Then add vanilla. Drop dough onto foil covered cookie sheet by the teaspoonful, 2 inches apart. Dough will spread during baking. Bake for 8 to 10 minutes. Cool cookie sheet on wire rack until foil removes easily. Remove foil from cookie sheet and place cookies on rack covered with absorbent paper to continue cooling. Makes 4 dozen cookies.

Submitted by Ron Haynes
Madison

MOM'S HEALTH COOKIES

My mom was always searching out recipes with a nutritional value that also passed the taste test. No empty calories for her or her family. This is her healthy crunchy, chewy cookie recipe. Serve with a bowl of fresh fruit or an apple or rhubarb sauce to equal a "nutrish and delish" dessert.

¼ cup canola oil
½ cup softened butter
½ cup brown sugar
½ cup pure Maine maple syrup
2 eggs
1 teaspoon vanilla extract
1 teaspoon baking powder
½ teaspoon baking soda
½ teaspoon salt
2 cups unbleached flour
2 cups rolled oats
3 cups cornflakes, wheat or bran flakes
½ cup craisins or raisins
½ cup nuts, chopped
½ cup chocolate chips (for fun)

Mix together all ingredients in order given. Roll into 1 inch balls, place on greased cookie sheet, and flatten with fork. Bake in 350 degree oven until golden. Makes about 3 dozen.

In memory of my dear mom, Wilma Gamage, who is responsible for my life-long determination to cook from scratch—most of the time—well-balanced and attractive meals that please the palate. She consistently used pure Maine maple syrup throughout her life. Her introduction to the real stuff began on her dad's family farm atop what is now Center Hill State Park in Weld.

OATMEAL COOKIES

Another yummy cookie packed with "good stuff"—pure Maine maple syrup, rolled oats, milk, eggs, raisins, nuts. This makes a soft cookie. They can't be beat!

½ cup butter
1 cup pure Maine maple syrup
½ cup milk
2 eggs
1½ cups flour
1 teaspoon salt
2 teaspoons baking powder
½ cup raisins
1½ cups rolled oats
½ cup chopped nuts (optional)

Preheat oven to 350 degrees. Beat butter, maple syrup, milk, and eggs together. Sift flour, salt, and baking powder. Add dry ingredients to wet ingredients and stir. Add raisins, rolled oats, and nuts. Drop by spoonfuls onto greased cookie sheet. Bake until browned. Makes 4 dozen.

Submitted by SMMSA

HERMITS

Adele Suga of Suga Country Products in Vassalboro likes to use recipes she feels are healthier for her and her husband.

"I'm always trying to find recipes that give Joe baked goods with less fat and sugar. Even though maple syrup is sugar, I'm convinced it's got to be better for us than white sugar. Here is an old favorite," offers Adele.

½ cup Smart Balance or Promise margarine
¾ cup pure Maine maple syrup
2 eggs
1¾ cups flour
1 teaspoon baking soda
¾ teaspoon salt
1 teaspoon cinnamon
½ cup raisins
1 cup rolled oats

Preheat oven to 375 degrees. Cream together margarine and maple syrup; beat in eggs. Combine flour, baking soda, salt, and cinnamon. Then slowly beat into creamed mixture. Stir in raisins and rolled oats. Drop by spoonfuls onto greased cookie sheet. Bake for 10 to 14 minutes. Makes approximately 3 dozen cookies.

Submitted by Adele Suga
Suga Country Products, Vassalboro

WHITE CHOCOLATE CHIP PECAN BROWNIES

This recipe makes an irresistible blond brownie—one of my favorites. The maple syrup simply, delicately mellows. However, I use 1 stick of butter and 1/3 cup canola oil in place of 2 sticks of butter. If I don't have the white chips and pecans in the cupboard, I use chocolate chips and walnuts.

2 sticks butter, softened to room temperature
1½ cups light brown sugar
2 eggs
2 teaspoons vanilla extract
½ cup pure Maine maple syrup
3 cups unbleached flour
Dash salt
1 teaspoon baking powder
2 cups white chocolate morsels
1 cup chopped pecans

Preheat oven to 350 degrees. Beat together butter and brown sugar until smooth. Beat in eggs until creamy. Add vanilla and maple syrup and beat. Sift flour, baking powder, and salt together and slowly add to mixture and mix until combined. Mix in morsels and pecans. Scrape into a greased and floured 9-inch square baking pan. Bake until set, about 20 to 30 minutes. Cool and cut into squares or bars. Makes 9 to 12 brownies.

A Chef Harry recipe

Harry Schwartz: television personality, author, and food columnist

4 OATMEAL SQUARES

These are enticing maple squares with oatmeal and maple; fit for the health food fan.

¾ cup pure Maine maple sugar or 2/3 cup white sugar
1 cup canola oil
2 teaspoons vanilla extract
1 cup pure Maine maple syrup
            (Dark or Extra Dark Amber)
2 eggs
2 cups Quick Rolled Oats
1 1/3 cups flour
1½ teaspoon baking powder
1 teaspoon salt
½ cup nuts, chopped (optional)

Preheat oven to 350 degrees. Mix ingredients in order and cream until smooth. Stir in nuts last and bake in greased 9 x 13 inch pan or jellyroll pan for about 30 minutes.

Submitted by Kristi Brannen
Spring Break Maple & Honey, Smyrna

MAPLE SYRUP SQUARES

Special for a special occasion.

Crust:

1½ cup flour
¼ cup moist brown sugar
½ cup butter

Filling:

1 cup moist brown sugar
1½ cup pure Maine maple syrup
3 eggs, beaten
3 tablespoons flour
¼ teaspoon salt
1 teaspoon vanilla extract

Preheat oven to 350 degrees. Prepare crust by mixing 1½ cups flour, ¼ cup brown sugar, and ½ cup butter until granular in texture. Press into a greased 9 x 13 inch pan. Bake until golden, about 10 to 15 minutes.

Meanwhile, prepare filling. Mix 1 cup brown sugar, 1½ cups maple syrup in saucepan and heat to boiling. Let simmer 5 minutes. Cool slightly. Pour in beaten eggs, stirring constantly. Then add 3 tablespoons flour, ¼ teaspoon salt and 1 teaspoon vanilla. Mix thoroughly. Pour onto baked crust. Bake for another 20 to 25 minutes.

Submitted by Surge Gilbert
Quebec

BAKLAVA

A favorite Greek treat with a Maine modification! "My baklava gets lots of 'ooohhs' and 'aaahhs' when I serve it," writes Kristi, owner of Spring Break Maple & Honey.

Syrup:

1 1/3 cups water
2/3 to ¾ cup pure Maine maple sugar
1 tablespoon lemon juice
1/3 cup pure Maine maple syrup, Dark or Extra Dark

Combine water, maple sugar, and lemon juice in saucepan. Bring to boil and boil, uncovered, for 10 minutes. Remove from heat and add maple syrup. Cool.

Baklava:

½ pound hazelnuts, chopped
½ pound pistachio nuts, chopped
½ cup pure Maine maple sugar
1 tablespoon cinnamon
2/3 cup sweet butter, melted
2/3 pound phyllo dough (Follow directions on package to use.)

Preheat oven to 325 degrees. Combine hazelnuts, pistachio nuts, maple sugar and cinnamon; set aside. Using a pastry brush, butter bottom of a sheet pan. Lay 8 sheets of phyllo dough, one at a time into it, brushing each with butter and sprinkling each with the nut mixture. Brush top sheet with butter. Cut into diamond shapes. Bake until phyllo starts to brown, (30 minutes). Lower heat to 300 degrees; continue to bake until golden. Pour *cooled* syrup onto *hot* baklava and cool at least 2 hours.

Submitted by Kristi Brannen
Spring Break Maple & Honey, Smyrna

PUDDING & PIE DESSERTS

(From the "slide-down easy" to the sticky and chewy)

APPLE CRUSTY

"I think I make the best apple crusty in my country. My secret? Pure Maine maple syrup!" writes Lisanne, a Maine maple producer from Quebec.

This dessert is so delicately delicious, it doesn't need a topping, but a dollop of whipped cream, vanilla yogurt or ice cream will dress it up, if you wish.

5 or 6 apples, peeled and sliced (or 4 cups)
½ to ¾ cup Pure Maine maple syrup
½ cup flour
½ cup rolled oats
¼ to ½ cup light brown sugar
¼ to ½ teaspoon salt
1/3 to ½ cup butter
½ teaspoon cinnamon (optional)
¼ teaspoon nutmeg (optional)

Preheat oven to 375 degrees. Arrange apple slices into a buttered 8-inch square pan and pour maple syrup over them. Mix flour, oats, brown sugar, and salt (spices, if desired). Cut in butter until mixture looks like small bread crumbs. Sprinkle over apples and syrup. Bake about 35 minutes.

Submitted by Lisanne Lapointe
Quebec

BAKED APPLES

Another heavenly maple-apple dessert! Also, it's nutritious and fat-free. Dress it up with a plop of fat-free frozen yogurt.

Apples, one for each serving
Pure Maine maple syrup or maple sugar
Ground cinnamon
Nuts, chopped (optional)
Raisins (optional)

Preheat oven to 375 degrees. Prepare 1 apple for each serving by washing and hollowing out the center. Be sure not to puncture the bottom of the apple. Fill the center with maple syrup or maple sugar. Nuts and/or raisins may be added. Sprinkle on a dash of cinnamon and bake until tender when pierced with fork, about 45 minutes.

FRESH FRUIT DESSERT

"One of my favorite recipes," writes Edwina.

This dish can also be served as a fresh fruit salad for brunch or lunch.

Wash and cut fresh fruit (apples, pears, oranges, kiwi, grapefruit, pineapple, berries, melon) into bite-sized pieces. Spoon into individual serving bowls. Mix sour cream and pure Maine maple syrup to taste and pour over the fruit.

Submitted by Edwina Hardy
Mountain Maple, Rumford

FRUIT UPSIDE-DOWN CAKE

Valentine's Day is always a special evening for a few couples in our town. The men traditionally plan and cook an elegant meal for their Valentine's. This past year John had refined his Whole Wheat Maine Maple Syrup Bread recipe for Maine Maple Beyond Pancakes, *and he agreed to provide bread for the Valentine's meal. Compliments flew, seconds were eaten.*
"John, what's your secret?" Dave, a friend, inquires.
"My maple syrup!" John boasts with no hesitation.
"Ah, maple syrup!" He turns to me. "You know, I bet an Apple Upside-Down Cake made with maple syrup would make a good recipe for your cookbook. My grandmother used to make one. Do you have a recipe for one of those yet?"
"Actually no, Dave," I answer. "Would you like to concoct one for me?"
We hear his daughter's voice from a distance. "Ya, Dad, you know how you love to mess around with recipes; always trying to make them better. Go for it!"
Seven months later Dave's gem appears in my mailbox:

Upside-down topping:

3 tablespoons butter
¼ cup pure Maine maple syrup
1 tablespoon brown sugar
¼ teaspoon cinnamon
1/3 cup chopped pecans (optional)
1½ cups sliced fruit (apples, peaches, pineapple, apricots),
         enough to cover the bottom of the pan with a single
         layer of fruit
Blackberries, raspberries, maraschino cherries for garnish,
    (optional)
Lemon juice

FRUIT UPSIDE-DOWN CAKE (continued)

Preheat oven to 350 degrees. Melt butter in 8-inch square pan as the oven heats. Remove from oven once the butter has melted and add maple syrup, brown sugar, cinnamon, and pecans to melted butter. Stir to mix. Add sliced fruit. Garnish with blackberries, raspberries, maraschino cherries, if desire. Drizzle with a bit of lemon juice.

Cake batter:

1¾ cups flour
1 teaspoon baking powder
½ teaspoon baking soda
½ teaspoon salt
¼ cup butter
¼ cup pure Maine maple syrup
½ cup sugar
2 eggs
¼ cup sour cream
1 teaspoon vanilla
1 teaspoon lemon zest

Sift together flour, baking powder, baking soda, and salt. Set aside. In separate bowl cream butter, maple syrup, and sugar; beat in eggs. Add sour cream, vanilla, and lemon zest. Mix until well blended. Then add dry ingredients, mix and spoon the stiff batter over the fruit upside-down topping. Bake at 350 degrees for about 30-35 minutes; test center with toothpick. Top should be a deep golden brown. Let cool on wire rack 10-15 minutes and then turn out onto a large serving platter. Serve warm topped with whipped cream.

Submitted by David Haynes, Yarmouth
Friend of Jackson Mountain Farm

GINGERBREAD

*Love traditional old-fashion gingerbread and whipped cream?
Try this treat with a new twist: ginger with Maine maple syrup
and sour cream. For a yummy idea transform the gingerbread and
whipped cream dessert into rhubarb shortcake. Just top a serving
of gingerbread with maple rhubarb sauce (see Index for recipe)
and whipped cream and devour. Yum!*

2 cups flour
½ teaspoon salt
1 teaspoon ginger
½ teaspoon cinnamon
¼ teaspoon cloves
1 teaspoon baking soda
½ cup pure Maine maple syrup
       (Medium or Dark Amber)
2 eggs, beaten
1 cup commercial sour cream (non-fat and low-fat work)

Preheat oven to 325 degrees. Sift together flour, salt, ginger,
cinnamon, cloves, and baking soda and set aside. Mix maple
syrup with beaten eggs; stir in sour cream. Add dry ingredients
and mix well. Bake in greased 8-inch square pan for 20 to 30
minutes. Serve warm with whipped cream.

BISCUIT DELIGHT

"My mother-in-law, Monique Wolcott, certainly has cooking talent to spare. She has offered this quick and delicious maple biscuit dessert."

Paul Rossignol
Nature's Sweetness: Pure Maple Syrup

2 cups all-purpose flour
1 tablespoon baking powder
½ teaspoon salt
¼ cup shortening
¾ cup milk
1½ cups pure Maine maple syrup

Preheat oven to 450 degrees. In a bowl combine flour, baking powder, and salt. Cut in shortening until mixture resembles coarse crumbs. Add milk and stir just until moistened. Turn onto lightly floured surface. Knead gently 4 to 5 times to form into a ball. Roll or pat to ½ inch thickness. Cut with a 2-inch biscuit cutter. Pour maple syrup into 11x 7 inch baking pan. Place biscuit on top of maple syrup. Bake for 10 to 15 minutes, until biscuits are golden.

From *Nature's Sweetness: Pure Maple Syrup* with permission.
Paul Rossignol, author and publisher, Topsham

SWEET ROLL PUDDING

"A Bacon Farm favorite that our family loves!" exclaims Shelley
Bacon.

3 cups cinnamon-raisin roll crumbs (about 2 to 3 rolls)
2 large eggs, lightly beaten
1½ cups milk
¾ cup sugar
1 teaspoon vanilla extract
¼ cup butter, melted
2 tablespoons pure Maine maple syrup
Caramel ice cream topping

Preheat oven to 300 degrees. Sprinkle 3 cups torn rolls into
lightly greased, shallow 1-quart baking dish. Combine eggs and
milk; stir in sugar and vanilla and turn onto torn rolls. Combine
butter and maple syrup and pour over all. Bake for 1 hour or
until golden. Serve with caramel topping. Serves 4 to 6.

Note: A 7.3 ounce size Pillsbury "poppin' fresh" refrigerated tube
of cinnamon rolls may be used in place of homemade cinnamon
rolls.

Submitted by Shelley Bacon
Bacon Farm Maple Products, Sidney

CUP CUSTARDS

The maple changes a long-time favorite custard recipe into a delicacy with a satiny texture. It slides down easily after a hearty meal and is a fun way to get a serving of the important dairy foods. Dress it up with fresh berries.

4 eggs
3 cups milk
¾ cup pure Maine maple syrup
Pinch of salt
¼ teaspoon vanilla extract
Sprinkles of nutmeg, if desired

Preheat oven to 350 degrees. Beat eggs slightly; add milk, maple syrup, salt and vanilla, then beat. Pour into 8 individual custard cups or 1½ quart baking dish and sprinkle with a little nutmeg. Set in a pan of hot water, and bake for about 45 minutes. Test doneness by inserting knife blade into center. If it comes out clean, the custard is done. Cool before serving.

 # BREAD PUDDING

7 slices whole-grain bread, broken into bite-sized pieces
3 cups scalded milk
2 beaten eggs
1 cup pure Maine maple syrup
¼ teaspoon salt
1 teaspoon cinnamon
½ cup raisins (optional)

Turn bread into buttered casserole. Mix remaining ingredients and pour over bread. Bake one hour in 350 degree oven. Serve warm with berries and whipped cream.

Submitted by SMMSA

CRÈME BRULEE

*I've always skipped over the Crème Brulee recipes; I guess,
because of the calories and cholesterol it packs and the long
narration of "how-to". It looked like a complicated process, but
my friend Val said, "Oh, yes, the maple cookbook must have a
Crème Brulee recipe. It's such a popular dessert these days, the
perfect ending to an elegant meal. " So I scanned my recipes,
modified the calories and cholesterol, read through the lengthy
directions, and started in. It was easier to make than I had
anticipated and was truly the "perfect ending". Elegant.
This is a make-a-day-ahead recipe. Serves two, but is easily
doubled or tripled.*

3 egg yolks
¼ cup pure Maine maple syrup
½ teaspoon vanilla extract
1 cup whipping cream
2 tablespoons light brown sugar

Preheat oven to 325 degrees. Heat 4 cups of water to boiling
and keep hot. Gently whisk together egg yolks, maple syrup,
and vanilla. Scald cream in heavy sauce pan over medium
heat. Gradually pour the hot cream into the egg yolk mixture,
stirring constantly, until well blended. Strain mixture into a large
measuring cup and pour into two custard cups. Place the cups
in baking dish and pour hot water half way up the outside of
cups. (Be careful not to splash water onto custards.) Cover
loosely with aluminum foil and bake between 50-60 minutes.
Remove from oven. Center of custards should be wobbly; they
will firm as they cool. Cool to room temperature, cover with
plastic wrap, and refrigerate overnight or up to 48 hours. An
hour before serving, remove from refrigerator. When ready to
serve, sprinkle one tablespoon of brown sugar over each cup
and place in baking dish. Pour ice water half way up the outside
of cups. Broil tops a minute or two, until sugar has caramelized.
Watch closely. Listen to your guests rave.

WARM MAPLE PUDDING

Doesn't this recipe sound too good not to try? I received three similar versions of this pudding, so it must be a very favorite. Serve warm with ice cream.

Maple Sugar Sauce (option #1):

2 cups pure Maine maple sugar
2 cups boiling water
1 tablespoon flour
Mix all together until blended, or make option #2

Maple Syrup Sauce (option #2):

¼ cup butter
¼ cup cornstarch
1½ cups pure Maine maple syrup
½ cup water

Melt butter and mix with corn starch. Add maple syrup and water and boil until it starts to thicken. Continue to cook 5 more minutes while stirring. Cool at least 15 minutes.

Batter for both options:

2 eggs
1 cup pure Maine maple sugar (white sugar will do)
1¼ cup flour
Dash salt
2 teaspoons baking powder
1 cup milk

Beat eggs, add sugar, and mix in flour, salt, and baking powder alternately with milk. Pour batter into 9 x 13 inch pan. Pour #1 or #2 sauce over batter and bake at 375 degrees for 30-40 minutes.

Submitted by Laurette Cameron and Surge Gilbert, Quebec, and the "hay man," Smyrna to surprise his mom, Enid McNealy, McNealy Farms, Gorham.

TOASTED ALMOND AND MAPLE PARFAIT

"This can be made a week in advance and stored in the freezer,"
Val offers. "Serve to expected—or unexpected—company."

6 ounces whole almonds (with skins)
¾ cup pure Maine maple syrup
1 quart vanilla ice cream, softened
¼ cup slivered almonds (for topping)

Preheat oven to 400 degrees. Spread whole almonds on baking
sheet and toast until golden brown, about 10 minutes. Shake
pan occasionally to turn nuts over. Cool. Grind nuts in food
processor and mix the ground nuts with maple syrup to make a
thin paste. (Add more syrup, if necessary.)

Spoon a generous amount of almond paste into the bottom of
eight 6-ounce parfait or wine glasses. Cover with a thick layer
of ice cream. Repeat the layers. Cover each glass securely with
plastic wrap and place in safe section of freezer.

Remove from freezer 30 minutes before serving. Garnish with
slivered almonds and a fresh strawberry or raspberry. Serves 8.

Submitted by Val Vaughan, Yarmouth
A former backyard Maine maple producer

FROZEN STRAWBERRY DESSERT

Kathy Lucas writes, "This recipe was given to me by Belle (Jackson) White, my dear friend and roommate at Farmington State Teachers College. In the early seventies we each had four children and often exchanged time-saving and make-ahead recipes. We had little time to peruse cookbooks.
This dessert can be made several days ahead. Enjoy!"

I bet fresh raspberries would work, too.

1¼ cups unbleached flour
¼ cup pure Maine maple syrup
1½ cups chopped walnuts
1½ cups melted butter
½ teaspoon vanilla extract
2 egg whites, separated from large eggs
½ cup sugar
2 teaspoons lemon juice
2 cups sliced strawberries, fresh or frozen
1 cup whipped cream

Preheat oven to 350 degrees. Mix flour, maple syrup, walnuts, melted butter, and vanilla together with fork until well blended. Spread in a 9 x 13 inch pan and bake 20 to 25 minutes. Stir twice while baking. Reserve 3 tablespoons for a topping. Then set aside the remaining mixture and cool completely. Meanwhile beat egg whites on high speed until stiff; add sugar gradually and beat. Add lemon juice and strawberries. Fold in whipped cream. (Mixture will be thick and creamy in appearance.) Spread strawberry mixture over cooled walnut mixture. Then sprinkle reserved mixture over top. Wrap well with plastic wrap and freeze for 6 hours. When ready to serve, remove from freezer and let set for 5 minutes. Return extra to freezer for another day.

Submitted by Kathleen (Buck) Lucas, Portland
Friend of Jackson Mountain Farm

ICE CREAM TREAT

"Without ice cream there would be darkness and chaos."

Don Kardong, marathoner and writer, Stanford University

"My wife, Belinda, loves to make homemade ice creams," writes Paul. "Here is her recipe for a delightful maple ice cream."

2 cups heavy cream
1 cup pure Maine maple syrup
4 egg yolks, beaten
1 teaspoon vanilla extract
¼ cup walnuts, chopped (optional)

Add heavy cream to ice cream maker. Mix according to manufacturer's instructions. Meanwhile, heat maple syrup and pour slowly over beaten egg yolks. Cook in upper part of double boiler (or over a pan of hot water on hot burner) stirring constantly until thick; cool. Add cooled syrup mixture to the cream and add vanilla. Blend well and add walnuts, if desired.

From *Nature's Sweetness: Pure Maple Syrup* with permission.
Paul Rossignol, author and publisher, Topsham

 # MILK SHAKE

Another delicious dessert contributing to the daily dairy ration.

½ cup pure Maine maple syrup
2 cups milk
1 pint vanilla ice cream, softened

Mix all ingredients in blender and serve at once.

Submitted by SMMSA

MAPLE SYRUP PIE

Below is the original recipe served at "Aux Anciens Canadians"
restaurant, noted for its authentic regional cuisine, during the
Quebec Winter Carnival in 2002.

"Mere words cannot do justice in attempting to describe this pie.
If you have any fondness for sweets, this is truly a heavenly treat,"
writes Paul Rossignol.

1¼ cup light brown sugar
1/3 cup pure Maine maple syrup
½ cup light cream (35 %)
2 teaspoons butter, room temperature
2 large eggs, room temperature
Crust for 1-crust pie

Preheat oven to 350 degrees. Line 9" pie plate with crust, prick,
and pre-bake 15 minutes; cool. Blend brown sugar, maple
syrup, cream, butter, and eggs in a blender until well mixed.
Pour into pie crust. Bake for about 45 minutes, until set. Serve
at room temperature with whipped cream.

From *Nature's Sweetness: Pure Maple Syrup* with permission.
Paul Rossignol author and publisher, Topsham

Variation:
Jocelyne Cloutier and Chantal Gilbert from Canada combine
1½ cups pure Maine maple syrup with 1 cup cream and thicken
it with 3 tablespoons of cornstarch diluted in ¼ cup cold water.
Then they boil the mixture for 2 minutes, stirring constantly, then
cool and pour into a baked pie crust. Add nuts to taste. "Very
good!" they exclaim.

Submitted by Jocelyne Cloutier and Chantal Gilbert
Quebec

MAPLE NUT PIE

*Another excellent recipe created by Jody Haynes, a former
New York City chef. It was published in the November 2002 issue
of* Gourmet. *The contrast of the sweet maple and tartness of the
vinegar transforms a standard nut pie into a distinctive nut pie.
Can be made 8 hours ahead and kept at room temperature.*

Crust for 9-inch pie shell: With baking rack in middle of oven
preheat oven to 375 degrees. Line pie plate with dough from
your favorite recipe (Jody recommends an all-butter pastry)
and chill 30 minutes. Lightly prick bottom and sides and bake
until pastry is pale golden, about 15 minutes. Remove pie shell
and cool about 20 minutes. Reduce oven to 350 degrees.
Meanwhile, mix filling.

¾ cup dried cranberries
½ cup pecans, coarsely chopped
½ cup walnuts, coarsely chopped
½ cup hazelnuts, coarsely chopped
¾ cup pure Maine maple syrup (Dark or Extra Dark)
½ cup packed dark brown sugar
¼ cup unsalted butter, melted
3 large eggs
2 tablespoons bourbon (optional)
1 teaspoon cider vinegar
1/8 teaspoon salt

Soak cranberries in 1 cup hot water until soft, about 10 minutes.
Drain well. Toast all nuts in 350 degree oven for about
6 minutes, until fragrant. Whisk together syrup, sugar, butter,
eggs, bourbon, vinegar, and salt. Stir in nuts and cranberries.
Pour into cooled pie shell; bake until set, 40 to 50 minutes. Cool
completely.

Submitted by Jody Haynes

SQUMPKIN PIE

Another recipe for a scrumptious pie served and sold at Yellow House Bed, Breakfast and Catering, in Oakfield. If you want to bake only a 9" pie, fill your pie shell to desired level and bake the rest of the filling in a casserole dish. It makes a simply divine squmpkin pudding. Jazz it up with a spoon of ice cream and sprinkle with nuts.

1 pie shell for 10 inch pie plate
½ cup light brown sugar
½ cup white sugar
1 tablespoon cornstarch
¾ teaspoon ginger
½ teaspoon cinnamon
½ teaspoon nutmeg
½ teaspoon salt
2 cups mashed squash (or 15 ounce can of pie filling)
1 cup mashed pumpkin (or ½ of 15 ounce can filling)
3 eggs, beaten
18 ounces canned evaporated milk
1½ tablespoons butter, melted
1 teaspoon lemon juice
½ tablespoon molasses
½ cup Maine maple syrup

Sift together sugars, cornstarch, ginger, cinnamon, nutmeg, and salt. In another bowl mix together squash and pumpkin. Add dry mixture to pumpkin and squash. Mix together eggs, milk, butter, lemon juice, molasses, and maple syrup. Add to squmpkin mixture and stir well. Set aside. Roll out pie crust and line 10-inch pie plate. Pour squmpkin filling into pie shell. Bake 20 minutes at 425 degrees, reduce heat to 350 degrees and bake an additional 1 hour, or until knife comes out clean when inserted into center of filling. Serve topped with ice cream or whipped cream.

Submitted by Gina Iacoponi Clark, Innkeeper/Chef
Yellow House Bed & Breakfast, Oakfield

PAPA GINO'S NEVER-FAIL PIE CRUST

For our very special maple pies, Gina, innkeeper and chef at the Yellow House Bed and Breakfast in Oakfield, shares her "baker-man" dad's never-fail pie crust recipe with us. It's not only never-fail, but so tender and flakey.

This recipe makes 4 crusts for two 9-inch pies or 3 crusts for three 10-inch single crust pies. If you do not want to make 2 or 3 pies, just store the extra crust, wrapped in individual baggies (one for each crust) in the freezer; or simply halve the recipe.

4 cups flour
1 tablespoon sugar
1 teaspoon salt
½ teaspoon baking powder
2 cups shortening (Papa Gino prefers Crisco)
1 cup ICE WATER

Sift flour, sugar, salt, and baking powder together into ice cold bowl. Add shortening and cut in with 2 table knives (not a pastry blender). Add ice water very slowly mixing with table fork to make a WET ball. Refrigerate ball for 2 hours, if you are planning to use the whole batch for pies at this baking session. Roll out crusts on floured board. Otherwise, divide into individual crust balls, place on cookie sheet and freeze. Then store in individual plastic bags in freezer.

Note: Balls need to be wet to touch. If they are dry and seemingly perfect texture, crust will crack when rolled. Thaw frozen balls in REFRIGERATOR. (I take them out of the freezer the night before I plan to make my pies.)

A SECRET TIP from Gino—"For the most beautiful golden baked pie, brush with a beaten whole egg.

IT'S EASY AS PIE!

MITCH'S MAPLE APPLE PIE

"Mitch makes all our pies for the holidays and any potluck suppers we attend. They are always a hit," boasts his wife, Penny.

7-8 tart Cortland apples, peeled, cored, and sliced
¾ cup pure Maine maple sugar
     or pure Maine maple syrup (Dark or Extra Dark)
Pinch salt
Pinch nutmeg
Couple shakes of cinnamon

Stir all together and put in refrigerator.

Crust:

3 cups flour
1 cup shortening
1 egg
Splash cider vinegar
3-4 tablespoons ice water

Preheat oven to 425 degrees. Cut shortening into flour. Mix egg, vinegar, and ice water together. Add to flour mixture. Work it in, adding more water if necessary, to form a ball. Roll out ½ of crust on floured board and line 10-inch pie plate. Dump in apple mixture, dot with butter. Then roll out remaining crust to cover apples and seal. Bake for 10 minutes at 425 degrees and reduce heat to 350 degrees and bake for about 30 or 40 minutes longer.

Submitted by Earle Mitchell
Mitchell and Savage Maple Syrup, Bowdoin

RHUBARB PIE

A blend of the very first crops of spring—maple syrup and rhubarb from down on the farm—will provide a delectable change from the soft winter pies. Dress it up with an oat topping and a scoop of vanilla ice cream.

Crust for 9-inch 2-crust pie; or, if choosing to make a one crust pie
    with oat topping, a 9-inch pie shell.
3-4 cups fresh rhubarb, cut into ½ inch pieces
¼ cup white sugar
½ cup pure Maine maple syrup
1 egg, beaten
½ teaspoon vanilla extract
3 tablespoons flour
1 tablespoon butter

Prepare crust and chill. Preheat oven to 425 degrees. Mix sugar with rhubarb; set aside while preparing topping, if using. Line pie plate with crust. Stir maple syrup, egg, vanilla, and flour into rhubarb and sugar. Turn into shell.
For 2-crust pie: Dot with butter and top with crust and seal. Bake for 40 to 50 minutes, until lightly browned and bubbling.
For 1-crust pie: Omit butter. Bake without topping for 20 minutes. Remove pie, reduce heat to 375 degrees, and add topping. Bake until juices bubble, another 30 to 40 minutes. Serve warm.

Oat Topping: Combine ½ cup rolled oats, ½ cup brown sugar, ½ cup flour, 1 tablespoon pure Maine maple syrup, 1/8 teaspoon cinnamon. Cut in ¼ cup butter.

An adaptation from *The Maple Syrup Cookbook*
by Ken Haedrich, and my mom's recipe

MAPLE CHEESECAKE

"This is great without any sauce or fruit; just let the pure maple flavor come out like a crown," raves Donna.

Crust:

2 cups honey graham crackers
¼ cup butter, melted
¼ cup pure Maine maple sugar or brown sugar

Combine all ingredients and press into 9-inch spring form pan. Set aside, or bake in 350 degree oven for 10 minutes.

Filling:

4 eggs, beaten
1 cup pure Maine maple syrup
24 ounces cream cheese, softened

1½ t vanilla
½ c. chopped pecans

Preheat oven to 350 degrees. Combine eggs, maple syrup, and cream cheese; beat until very smooth. Pour into crust and bake 60 minutes. Chill for several hours before serving.

Submitted by Donna Tracy
Maple Hill Farm, Farmington, ME

A yummy variation for filling PRALINE CHEESECAKE: Substitute 1¼ cup brown sugar for the maple syrup, add 2 tablespoons of flour, and 24 ounces cream cheese and mix until well blended. Beat in 3 to 4 eggs, one at a time. Blend in 1½ teaspoons vanilla extract and ½ cup finely chopped pecans. Bake at 350 degrees for 50 t0 55 minutes. Chill several hours. To serve, cover with pure Maine maple syrup. Garnish with pecan halves.

Submitted by Katherine Benson
Gorham

XI

MAPLE NIBBLES

Maine maple nibbles are not only praised for their delicate, delectable, delightful taste, they lift your spirit. Several are loaded with nutrition, and all provide ample exercise for finger, wrist, and jaw.

Also, they make attractive gifts any time of year. Just wrap in plastic baggies and tie with colorful ribbon, or fill a glass jar with screw-on lid. Tie a ribbon around the neck. They sell well at the church or local fund-raising food tables, too.

Nibbles are just plain family fun to make and to eat. Indulge! And remember to exercise afterward, too. It's the pure Maine maple syrup that makes the difference. Indulge! And remember to exercise afterwards.

"Grandma stood by the brass kettle and with the big wooden spoon, she poured hot syrup on each plate of snow. It cooled into soft candy, and as fast as it cooled they ate it. They could eat all they wanted, for maple sugar never hurt anybody."

Laura Ingalls Wilder
Little House in the Big Woods

MAPLE BRITTLE

A nutty, naturally sweet nibble—dip your fingers in after lunch, on the road, or package it for holiday gifts.

1 cup walnuts, pecans, or almonds
2 cups pure Maine maple syrup
2 tablespoons butter (not margarine)
¼ teaspoon cream of tartar

Spread nuts on a lightly buttered cookie sheet. Combine maple syrup, butter, and cream of tartar in pan. Boil to 280 degrees on candy thermometer, or until syrup forms a very hard thread in cold water. DO NOT STIR THE SYRUP or sugar crystals will form. Pour over nuts. Let cool. Break into pieces.

Submitted by Diane Haulk
Haulk's Maple, Madison

MAPLE TOASTED WALNUTS

Another sweet treat sure to please— "Sticky, but yummy!" shares Diana. Not only good for nibbling, but they are delish tossed onto a green salad or to top your ice cream or cake. The recipe does not include quantities; suit your fancy—a lot or a little.

Chop walnuts coarsely. Soak in pure Maine maple syrup, the darker the grade the better. Spread in a layer on a buttered baking sheet. Bake 20 minutes in 325 degree oven. Cool before serving.

Submitted by Diana Demers
Brambleberry Farm, Weld

MAPLE-COVERED NUTS

A nutritious snack sure to put smiles on the faces.
Would these taste yummy on a green salad? I bet.

1 pound of whole walnuts, almonds, or pecans
1 cup pure Maine maple syrup

Warm nuts to 200 degrees in oven. In medium-sized pan heat maple syrup to 235 degrees on candy thermometer. When syrup reaches temperature, stir in warmed nuts until they are well coated. Spread nuts on a buttered cookie sheet to cool, stirring every so often. When dry and cool, separate them and store in an airtight container.

Submitted by Donna Tracy
Maple Hill Farm, Farmington

PRALINES

Allergic to nuts? Try these.
A great treat for the lunchbox.

2 cups pure Maine maple syrup
1 tablespoon butter or ¼ cup cream
1½ cup quick oats

Boil in large pan, maple syrup and cream (or butter) to 233 degrees or until a firm ball forms when dropped in cold water. Remove from heat and add oats. Cool slightly. Then drop by spoonfuls onto waxed paper.

Submitted by University of Maine Cooperative Extension
Bangor

MAPLE POPCORN & NUTS

This nibble will disappear like magic! It will quickly become a favorite in front of the television, at any gathering! Simply enjoy.

9 cups popcorn or 1/3 cup raw popcorn, popped
1 cup salted peanuts or mixed nuts
1 cup pure Maine maple syrup
1 cup white sugar
½ teaspoon white vinegar
2 tablespoons butter

Preheat oven to 200 degrees. Turn popped corn and nuts into buttered roasting pan and mix.

Heat maple syrup, sugar, and vinegar to boil in a heavy medium-sized saucepan, stirring to dissolve sugar. Cook, WITHOUT STIRRING, to 240 degrees on candy thermometer, or until syrup forms a long thread when dropped into cold water. Add butter and stir until melted. Pour over popcorn and nuts. Toss gently.

Bake 1 hour. Cool, and then break apart to form chunks. Store in air tight container or plastic bags.

Keeps well in the freezer, also, for a make ahead treat. Makes 9 to 10 cups.

Submitted by Pat Jillson
Jillson's Farm Stand, Sabattus

MAPLE KISSES

"Maple kisses are as sweet as they sound," brags Paul Rossignol, who enjoys making these treats with his daughters, Shelby and Renee.

2 cups sugar
2/3 cup pure Maine maple syrup
¾ cup water
1 teaspoon vanilla extract
¾ cup walnuts, coarsely broken

Stir together sugar, syrup, and water in a heavy sauce pan. Cook, stirring until sugar is dissolved (soft ball stage—240 degrees). Cool until lukewarm. Then beat until creamy. Stir in vanilla and nuts. Drop from tip of spoon into small rough heaps onto a greased cookie sheet to cool. Serve with a hug and smile.

From *Nature's Sweetness/Pure Maple Syrup* with permission.
Paul Rossignol, author and publisher, Topsham

MAPLE SUGAR ON SNOW
(MAPLE TAFFY)

Making taffy is an old traditional New England custom during sugaring time. It is traditionally served with doughnuts and sour pickles. Great fun for family and friends!

2 cups pure Maine maple syrup (Light Amber)

Boil on medium-high heat to 235 degrees in 4-quart pot. Pour immediately onto a mound of clean, fresh snow. Wind on fork or indulge with fingers to eat. Serves 7 to 8 people.

Submitted by University of Maine Cooperative Extension
Bangor

MAPLE FUDGE

Everyone loves a nibble of fudge. This is rich and creamy tasting fudge that is naturally sweet with the delicateness of pure maple. Once sampled—irresistible! Addicting!

"This recipe has made its way from Canada, to Maine, to Virginia, to North Carolina, to Alaska, to Ontario; and is welcomed wherever it goes!" exclaims Diana. So-o-o folks, give it a try.

2 cups pure Maine maple syrup
               (Light or Medium Amber)
1 tablespoon light corn syrup
Shake of salt (optional)
¾ cup light cream
1 teaspoon vanilla extract
¾ cup walnuts, coarsely chopped (optional)

Combine maple syrup, corn syrup, shake of salt (if using), and cream in a 3-quart saucepan. Bring to boil over low heat, stirring constantly. Continue cooking WITHOUT STIRRING to the softball stage (235 to 240 degrees). Remove from heat. Cool to lukewarm. Beat mixture until it thickens and looses its gloss. Add vanilla and nuts, if using. Pour into an 8-inch square buttered pan or candy molds. Cool and cut. Enjoy!

Submitted by Diana Demers
Brambleberry Farm, Weld

Laurette Cameron from Quebec says she substitutes 1 cup sugar for the corn syrup and uses 1 cup of cream instead of ¾ cup.

XII

PANCAKES, WAFFLES, & FRENCH TOAST

Favorite foods for a leisurely meal to be shared with family
and friends and served with the favored, delectable, delicious
topping—pure Maine maple from our own Maine maple producers.

MUSINGS
(flat cakes cooked in a pan)

No dough to knead, no tearing crust,
But Maine maple syrup is a must!

Thin ones, fluffy ones,
Even old-fashioned ones,
Healthy, hearty, favorite ones!
Berry ones, apple ones,
Banana, nutty, pumpkin ones!
And ones flipped just for fun!

Ones with sweet milk, ones with buttermilk,
And ones made with spelt.

Ones for breakfast, ones for lunch,
Ones for supper, and ones for brunch.

What? Ones for dessert?
You bet!!!

I know you must have a favorite recipe; it may even be from a box.
However, I've included a few of our favorites to revitalize your
from scratch-made cakes. Give them a try.

OLD-FASHIONED PANCAKES

"My brother, Gene, claims that this is the best pancake recipe, period. This is my mother, Claudette's recipe that we grew up enjoying. Serve the cakes with granulated maple sugar sprinkled on top and plenty of maple syrup, and eat them in the company of family. Life is good!"

Nature's Sweetness/Pure Maple Syrup

3 eggs, well-beaten
2 cups milk
½ teaspoon salt
2 to 2 ½ cups flour
1 teaspoon white sugar
5 teaspoons baking powder

Mix together eggs and milk. In another bowl mix salt, flour, sugar, and baking powder. (If using whole wheat flour, use the lesser amount of flour.) Combine the two mixtures until dampened. DO NOT BEAT. Mixture will be lumpy.
Spoon onto griddle, making individual cakes the size of your choice. Or be imaginative and create snowmen for the younger ones. Cook until small bubbles start to form within the cakes. Flip, only once and finish cooking. Makes about 12 pancakes.

From *Nature's Sweetness/Pure Maple Syrup* with permission.
Paul Rossignol, author and publisher, Topsham

Hints For Perfect Pancakes:

Extra liquid equals thinner pancakes; more flour thickens them.
Do not beat. Stir only enough to moisten batter.
Flip pancakes once, just as bubbles start to appear in the
        cooking pancakes.

LEE'S FAVORITE PANCAKES

These light and puffy pancakes, adorned with pure Maine maple syrup, of course, will be the rave of the morning. Toss in Maine blueberries, raspberries or sliced Maine apples or peaches to please the palate and to add crunch, color, and nutrition. During strawberry season dress the pancakes with freshly sliced strawberries before topping them with maple syrup. Oh, what a treat!

2 cups flour
1 teaspoon baking soda
¼ cup sugar
¼ teaspoon salt
4 eggs, separated
¼ cup oil
1 cup buttermilk (or sour milk)
1 to 2 cups of blueberries, raspberries, or thinly sliced apples or
        peaches (optional)

Sift together flour, baking soda, sugar, and salt; set aside. In another bowl beat egg whites until stiff. In a third bowl combine egg yolks, oil, and buttermilk and add to dry ingredients. Mix only until fully moistened. Add blueberries, raspberries, apples, or peaches, if using. Fold in egg whites. Cook at 325 degrees on electric griddle. Top with pure Maine maple syrup. Makes about 12 pancakes.

Submitted by Gwen Kinney
Kinney's Maple Supplies, Knox

Note: You can make pancakes with this recipe without separating the eggs. The pancakes just won't be as light and fluffy.

SPELT PANCAKES

Spelt, a native grain to southern Europe and western Asia, is a relatively new wheat grain to come to Maine. Penny says that spelt is a more soluble grain with less gluten, and therefore, our bodies asorb the nutrients more readily. It has a sweeter taste than whole wheat flour. She and her husband, Mitch, grow it on their working farm.

1 cup spelt flour
1 teaspoon baking powder
½ teaspoon salt (optional)
1 tablespoon pure Maine maple syrup
1 egg, beaten
3 tablespoons oil or melted butter
1 cup milk

Sift together flour, baking powder, and salt. Add maple syrup, egg, oil, and milk and stir only enough to thoroughly blend the ingredients. Cook on medium-hot griddle. Top with pure Maine maple syrup. Makes about 6 pancakes.

Submitted by Penny Savage
Mitchell and Savage Maple Syrup, Bowdoin

187

BETHEL'S OATMEAL PANCAKES OR WAFFLES

Looking for a hearty and healthy pancake/waffle recipe? This is one. The oats provide an extra chew. (My daughter, Bethel, consistently cooks with whole-grains to boost nutrition and fiber into four growing sons.) Top with fresh berries or peaches and pure Maine maple syrup and the platter will be empty—bingo!

Don't have any bacon or sausage on hand to complement the meal? Grab the peanut butter jar and slather the peanut protein over the layers before you top with pure Maine maple syrup, a habit my brothers and I, as kids, learned "pigging-out" at the Sunday night suppers in Litchfield. What a marriage—peanut butter and pure maple syrup!

3 cups milk, scalded
2 cups rolled oats
3 eggs, separated
2 tablespoons canola oil or melted butter
1 cup whole wheat flour or unbleached flour
1½ tablespoons baking powder
¼ teaspoon salt

Scald milk and pour over oats measured into a medium-sized bowl. Cool for 30 minutes. Add egg yolks, oil, flour, baking powder, and salt and mix until ingredients are moistened. Beat egg whites until stiff. Fold into batter. Cook on griddle or waffle iron. Makes about 12 pancakes or 4 waffles.

An adaptation from *Cabbage Town Café Cookbook*
Bethel's favorite Ithaca café

BANANA FRITTERS

"My husband boarded with a lady in Gorham while going to college. She often made these for Sunday supper for the boys who lived there," writes Katherine.

Those were the "good ole days," right?

1½ cups flour
2 teaspoons baking powder
½ teaspoon salt
2 tablespoons sugar
2 tablespoons butter, melted
2 eggs, beaten
¾ cup milk
6 bananas, cut into ½ inch slices

Heat fat to 375 degrees for deep fat frying in a heavy pan or deep fat fryer. The melted fat should be 3 to 4 inches deep. Meanwhile, combine flour, baking powder, and salt and set aside. Mix together sugar and butter, add eggs, and then milk. Add to dry ingredients. Fold in sliced bananas.
Test fat with a candy thermometer, or drop a cube of white bread into the hot fat. If hot enough, it should brown in 40 seconds. When fat is hot, drop the batter by tablespoons into it. Cook until brown. Drain well on paper towel. Serve with pure Maine maple syrup. Lip-smackin' good!

Submitted by Katherine Y. Benson
Gorham

PUMPKIN WAFFLES

Recycle the Halloween pumpkin! The flesh is packed with lots of nutrition, you know.

These waffles are superb. I served them with sausage and fresh fruit, and, of course, topped with pure Jackson Mountain Farm maple syrup to friends for Sunday night supper before our weekly bridge game. We almost missed our game; we just kept eating and eating.

2 cups unbleached flour
1 cup whole wheat flour
1 tablespoon baking powder
3/8 teaspoon cinnamon
3/8 teaspoon ginger
3/8 teaspoon nutmeg
½ teaspoon salt
4 eggs, beaten
2 ½ cups milk
1 1/8 cup pumpkin pulp, mashed
¾ cup canola oil
½ cup walnuts, chopped (optional)

Preheat waffle iron. Sift together flours, baking powder, cinnamon, ginger, nutmeg and salt. In another bowl mix together eggs, milk, pumpkin, and oil. Add dry ingredients and nuts, if desired. Mix until well moistened. Bake in hot waffle iron. Makes 12 sections.
Serves 4 to 6.

Adapted from *Zucchini Cookbook*
Nancy Ralston and Marynor Jordan

POTATO WAFFLES

Leftover mashed potato in the refrigerator? A perfect recipe for a "second preparation". The munchers at the table will never recognize them. These potato waffles are fluffy and light. Topped with pure Maine maple syrup makes them even better.

1 teaspoon salt
3 cups flour
2¼ teaspoons sugar
2 teaspoons baking powder
1 teaspoon baking soda
4 eggs, separated
3 cups buttermilk (or sour milk)
1 cup mashed potato
¾ cup butter, melted

Preheat waffle iron. In a large mixing bowl, combine salt, flour, sugar, baking powder, and baking soda. Add egg yolks, buttermilk, and potatoes and mix until moistened. Add the butter. Beat the egg whites in a separate bowl until stiff. Gently stir them into the batter, and bake in the hot waffle iron. Serves 4.

Leftover waffles? Use them as bread to make a favorite sandwich.

STRAWBERRY SHORTCAKE WAFFLES

A dessert to live for!

Place waffle on plate, add a scoop of vanilla ice cream. Mound with sliced strawberries and drizzle with pure Maine maple syrup. Dig in!

CINNAMON FRENCH TOAST

Lure the family and overnight guests out of bed with the aroma of vanilla and cinnamon flavored French toast cooking on the griddle. Enhanced with pure Maine maple syrup as a topping, it will bring compliments galore!

Serve with fresh fruit salad and ham slices or sausage.

4 eggs
¾ cup skim milk
1 teaspoon vanilla extract
1 teaspoon cinnamon
¼ teaspoon nutmeg
8 slices whole-grain bread
Pure Maine maple syrup

Preheat griddle on medium heat. With fork or wire whisk, beat eggs in a shallow dish until foamy. Add milk, vanilla, cinnamon, and nutmeg. Beat well with whisk or fork. Soak each slice on both sides in mixture and cook on griddle, turning once, until golden.

FRENCH TOAST SANDWICH

Get fun and fancy. Serve French toast as a fresh berry sandwich. Drizzle a couple tablespoons of pure Maine maple syrup over 1½ cups raspberries and 2 cups sliced strawberries; set aside while cooking the French toast. To serve place one slice of toast on plate, spoon berries over it, and top with a second slice. Dust with confectioners' sugar and drizzle Maine maple syrup over all. YUM!

STUFFED BLUEBERRY FRENCH TOAST

An interested customer, who obviously likes to eat and share delicious foods, slid this recipe onto Eric Ellis' desk just before leaving Maine Maple Products, Inc. one day. He comments to Eric, "It's delicious with extra maple syrup poured over it when hot. And, it's just as good if you make half the recipe."

So, if you need a hearty and luscious dish for brunch that you can prepare the night before and pop into the oven the next morning, here it is.

12 slices white bread, cubed
2—8 ounce packages cream cheese cut into small cubes (or less)
1 cup blueberries, fresh or frozen (or more)

Butter an 8-inch by 10-inch roasting pan. Layer half of the bread cubes, all the cream cheese and all of the berries. Top with the rest of the bread cubes.

2 cups milk
12 eggs
1/3 cup pure Maine maple syrup

Mix together milk, eggs, and maple syrup. Pour over the ingredients in the pan. Cover and let sit over night in the refrigerator. Bake in a 350 degree oven, covered, for a half hour. Then uncover for a half hour longer; or until it is set. Splash with Maine maple syrup.

Submitted by Eric Ellis
Maine Maple Products, Madison

INDEX

Appetizers,
  dips,
    clam, 43
    fruit, 42
    Maine Maple Sunday, 43
    tomato, 41
    veggie, 42
  grapefruit, mapled, 44
  sausage appetizers, 44
  scallops, bacon-wrapped, 40
Apples
  apple and carrots, 119
  apple crusty, 158
  baked, 159
  cabbage and apple, 118
  pie, Mitch's maple apple, 175
  sauce, 28
  upside-down cake, 160
Baby Back Ribs, 86
Baked Beans
  Boston, 106
  ginger, 108
  quick, 109
Baklava, 157
Banana Fritters, 189
Beets, Harvard, 126
Beverages
  cider, Leslie's and
    Walt's mulled, 48
  cocktail, maple, 50
  cream soda, 48
  kahlua, 51
  lemonade, dog-day, 47
  mead, maple, 52
  milk, maple, 46

Beverages, (continued)
  punch, sugar-time, 47
  switchell, Mitchel, 46
  tea, maple chai, 49
Biscuit Delight, 163
Biscuits
  dropped, 75
  maple-topped, 76
Breads
  biscuits, see Biscuits
  blueberry walnut, 82
  coffee cake, rhubarb, 83
  cornbread, 70
  French toast, see
    French toast
  fritters, banana, 189
  johnnycake, 70
  muffins, see Muffins
  pancakes, see Pancakes
  scones, see Scones
  waffles, see Waffles
  zucchini, 80
  sweet breads
    blueberry walnut, 82
    zucchini, 80
  yeast breads
    meal-in-a-loaf, 64
    seven-grain, 61
    white, 60
    whole-wheat, 62
  yeast rolls
    bran, 66
    maple walnut, 68
    potato, 65

Brownies, white chocolate chip and pecan, 154
Cabbage
    cabbage and apples, 118
    salad with apples, 131
    slaw, Bethel's calico 130
Cakes and Frostings, Icings
    birthday cake, 143
    buttercup squash, 145
    carrot, 144
    coffee cake, rhubarb, 83
    loaf, 142
    upside-down, fruit, 160
Candies and nuts
    brittle, 179
    fudge, 183
    kisses, 182
    nuts, covered, 180
    nuts, maplized, 180
    popcorn and nuts, 181
    pralines, 180
    sugar on snow, 182
    taffy, 182
    walnuts, toasted, 179
Carrots
    baked with apples, 119
    cake, 144
    glazed, 119
Cereals
    granola, holiday, 58
    oatmeal,
      baked, 56
      maple cranberry, 55
      Swiss breakfast, 57
Cheesecake
    maple, 177
    praline, 177

Chicken
    maple cider, 98
    maple and ginger, 96
    orange maple sauce, 30
    orange thyme, 98
    pasta, Italian garden, 115
    peachy maple, 97
    roasted
      with rice, 102
      with vegetables, 100
    stir-fry, 103
    sweet and sour, 101
Chili, 110
Crystallization, 19
Comparing maple with white sugar, 15
Containers, 17
Converting recipes, 15
Cookies and squares
    baklava, 157
    brownies, white chocolate chip and pecan, 154
    healthy, 151
    hermits, 153
    lace, 150
    squares, see squares,
    oatmeal, dropped, 152
    sugar, 149
    Whoopie Pie, 148
Cornbread, 70
Cranberry sauce, 28
    orange-ginger, 29
Dips
    fruit, 42
    Maine Maple Sunday, 43
    tomato, 41
    vegetable, 42

Desserts
  apples, baked, 159
  apple crusty, 158
  baklava, 157
  biscuit delight, 163
  bread pudding, 165
  cakes, see Cakes
  cheesecake
    maple, 1177
    praline, 177
  cookies, see Cookies
  crème brulee, 166
  custard, 165
  fruit dessert, 159
  gingerbread, 162
  grapefruit, 44
  ice cream, 170
  milk shake, 170
  parfait, toasted almond
    and maple, 168
  pies, see Pies
  puddings
    bread, 165
    sweet roll, 164
    warm maple, 167
  squares,
    baklava, 157
    brownies, white chocolate
      chip and pecan, 154
    maple syrup, 156
    oatmeal, 155
  upside-down cake, fruit, 160
  strawberry dessert, frozen, 169
  waffle shortcake, 191
Eggplant and Summer Squash, 124
Farfalle, 114
Fish, see seafood

French Toast
  Cinnamon, 192
  Sandwich, 192
  stuffed blueberry, 193
Fritters, Banana, 189
Frostings, Icings, Whipped Cream
  frostings
    butter, 146
    cream cheese, 146
  icing
    boiled, 147
    quick, 147
  whipped cream, 147
Fudge, 183
Gingerbread, 162
Glazes
  maple-dijon for meatloaf, 31
  orange-maple, 30
Grading of syrup, 16
Granola, 58
Grapefruit, 44
Haddock, Baked, 95
Ham,
  baked, 91
  boiled, 91
  grilled, 90
History of maple syrup making, 24
Ice Cream Treat, 170
Introduction, 9
Jalapeno Baby Back Ribs, 86
Johnnycake, 70
Kahlua, 51

Main Dishes,
  baked beans
    Boston, 106
    ginger, 108
    quick, 109
  chicken
    roasted with vegetables, 100
    stir-fry, 103
    sweet and sour, 101
    with rice, 102
  chili, 110
  farfalle, 114
  pork and veggie medley, 112
  soup, cream of squash, 111
  stir-fry, vegetarian, 113
Maple Savvy, 13
  buying, where and when, 19
  crystallization, 19
  comparisons (maple with
    white sugar), 5
  containers, 17
  converting recipes, 5
  grading, 6
  introduction, 9
  making of, 22
  maple advantage
    (food value), 14
  mold, 18
  storing of, 18
  value-added products, 19
Meat Rub, 85
Milk Shakes, 170
Muffins
  bran, 71
  carrot, 73
  multi-grain, 72
  old-fashioned, 74

Nuts
  covered nuts, 180
  maplized nuts, 133
  popcorn and nuts, 181
  toasted walnuts, 179
Oatmeal
  baked, 56
  maple cranberry, 55
  pancakes, 188
  Swiss breakfast, 57
Onions, baked, 118
Orange syrup, 128
Pancakes
  favorite, Lee's, 186
  oatmeal, Bethel's, 188
  old-fashioned, 185
  spelt, 187
Pasta Dishes
  farfelle, 114
  Italian garden, 115
Pies
  apple, Mitch's maple, 175
  crust, Papa Gino's 174
  maple nut, 172
  maple syrup, 171
  rhubarb, 176
  squmpkin, 173
Popcorn and Nuts, 181
Pork
  pulled pork, 89
  tenderloin, maple-glazed, 87
  tenderloin, maple-mustard, 88
  spare ribs, 90
  veggie medley with pork, 112
Pumpkin,
  pie, squmpkin, 173
  waffles, 190

Rhubarb
  coffee cake, 83
  pie, 176
  sauce, 34
Rolls, yeast
  bran, 66
  maple walnut, 68
  potato, 65
Salads
  bean and corn, 136
  broccoli, 135
  cabbage and apple, 131
  citrus, 129
  mushroom, 132
  salmon, 137
  slaw, Bethel's calico, 130
  spinach and apple, 134
  spinach and pear, 133
  Waldorf, 128
Salad Dressings
  dijon-bacon, 138
  quick, for greens, 139
  tomato dip/dressing, 41
  tomato ketchup, 140
  vinaigrette, 139
Salmon
  broiled, maple-mustard, 92
  glazed, grilled, 94
  salad, 137
  teriyaki, 93

Sauces
  apple, 28
  BBQ sauce, 32
  berry, 35
  caramel, 36
  chocolate, 36
  cranberry, 28
  cranberry-orange-ginger, 29
  maple-mustard barbecue, 32
  maple walnut, 33
  orange-maple, 30
  peach, 35
  peanut butter, 34
  pineapple, 31
  rhubarb, 34
Scones
  maple nut, 77
  maple walnut and oatmeal, 78
Seafood
  haddock, 95
  salad, salmon, 137
  salmon, see Salmon,
  scallops, bacon-wrapped, 40
Soup, cream of squash, 111
Spreads
  cream cheese, 38
  Maine Maple Sunday, 43
  maple cream, 38
  maple butter, 37
  maple-honey, 37
Squash
  baked, 117
  cake, 145
  pie, squmpkin, 173
  summer, with eggplant, 124
  soup, cream of, 111

Steak, marinated London Broil, 85
Stir-fry
    chicken and vegetable, 103
    summer veggies, 125
    vegetarian, 113
Sweet Breads
    blueberry, 82
    zucchini, 80
Sweet potato
    candied, 121
    casserole, 122
    spears, 120
    with brussels sprouts, 123
    with roasted chicken, 100
Sweet and Sour Chicken, 101
Toppings
    maple syrup, 27
    maple walnut, 33
    orange syrup, 128
    whipped cream, 147
    see Glazes, Sauces, Spreads,
Vegetables
    beets, Harvard, 126
    brussels sprouts with
      sweet poatoes, 123

Vegetables (continued)
    cabbage and apples, 118
    carrots,
      baked with apples, 119
      glazed, 119
    eggplant and
      summer squash, 124
    onions, baked, 118
    summer veggies, stir-fry, 113
    squash
      glazed, 117
      summer, with eggplant, 124
    sweet potato,
      candied, 121
      casserole, 122
      spears, 120
      with brussels sprouts, 123
      with roasted chicken, 100
Vegetarian Stir-fry, 113
Waffles
    oatmeal, 188
    potato, 191
    pumpkin, 190
    strawberry shortcake, 191